This short book is a study of the epic tradition of the early Roman empire and specifically of the epic poems of Ovid, Lucan, Statius, Valerius Flaccus and Silius Italicus. It explores the use they made of Virgil's *Aeneid*, an epic interpreted not just as a monument to the heroic construction of the principate, but also as a problematical text that challenged succeeding epic poets to a reworking of the issues that it dramatized: the possibility of establishing a lasting age of peace, the relation between power and the sacred, the difficulties of distinguishing between good and its evil parodies, anxiety about imperial and poetic succession. The author draws on modern critical and theoretical approaches to argue for the vitality and interest of works which have all too often been relegated to a second division of literary history. He argues that these epics may in some ways be understood better through a forward rather than a backward glance, to the epics of the Middle Ages and Renaissance.

The book will be of interest to students of English epic and of comparative literature as well as to classicists. All Latin is translated.

ROMAN LITERATURE
AND ITS CONTEXTS

The epic successors of Virgil

ROMAN LITERATURE AND ITS CONTEXTS

Series editors:
Denis Feeney and Stephen Hinds

The editors of this series share the growing belief that the dominant modes of study of Roman literature are insufficiently in touch with current research in other areas of the classics and in the humanities at large. Students of Greek literature, in the best traditions of classical scholarship, have been strengthening their contacts with cognate fields such as social history, anthropology, history of thought, linguistics and literary theory; the study of Roman literature has just as much to gain from engaging with these other contexts and intellectual traditions. The series is designed to encourage readers of Latin texts to sharpen their readings by placing them in broader and better-defined contexts, and to encourage other classicists to explore the general or particular implications of their work for readers of Latin texts. The books all constitute original and innovative research and are envisaged as suggestive essays whose aim is to stimulate debate.

The epic successors
of Virgil

A study in the dynamics
of a tradition

Philip Hardie

University Lecturer in Classics,
University of Cambridge,
and Fellow of New Hall

CAMBRIDGE
UNIVERSITY PRESS

Published by the Press Syndicate of the University of Cambridge
The Pitt Building, Trumpington Street, Cambridge CB2 1RP
40 West 20th Street, New York NY 10011-4211, USA
10 Stamford Road, Oakleigh, Victoria 3166, Australia

First published 1993

Printed in Great Britain at the University Press, Cambridge

A catalogue record for this book is available from the British Library

Library of Congress cataloguing in publication data
Hardie, Philip R.
The epic successors of Virgil: a study in the dynamics of a tradition / by Philip Hardie.
p. cm. – (Roman literature and its contexts)
Includes bibliographical references and index.
ISBN 0–521–41542–X (hardback). – ISBN 0–521–42562–X (paperback)
1. Epic poetry, Latin – History and criticism. 2. Influence (Literary, artistic, etc.).
3. Imitation (in literature). 4. Virgil – Influence. 5. Virgil. Aeneid.
I. Title. II. Series.
PA6054.H28 1993
873′.0109–dc20 91–46846 CIP

ISBN 0 521 41542 X hardback
ISBN 0 521 42562 X paperback

For
Susan and the twins

Contents

Preface

This is a short book on some very long poems written in the first 130 years of the Roman empire: Ovid's *Metamorphoses*, Lucan's *Bellum Ciuile*, Statius' *Thebaid*, Valerius Flaccus' *Argonautica*, and Silius Italicus' *Punica*. My aim above all is to throw light on the dynamics of a tradition. Tradition is often felt negatively as a dead weight; I shall have succeeded if I encourage in my reader a sense that these monstrous poems are possessed of a restless and fertile energy and that close to the surface of their hides there is stretched an intricately sensitive nerve-system.

In literary terms the source of this dynamism is Virgil's *Aeneid*. One of the greatnesses of this apparently definitive Roman epic is its ability to spawn a vigorous progeny. The successors to Virgil, at once respectful and rebellious, constructed a space for themselves through a 'creative imitation' that exploited the energies and tensions called up but not finally expended or resolved in the *Aeneid*. In historical terms epic flourished because it answered to many of the political and ideological concerns of the first century A.D. Epic and the empire share a number of obsessions: the search, never fulfilled, for a final perfection and equilibrium amidst the instabilities of power; the difficulty of distinguishing between good and evil; anxiety about the succession. Repetition, witting and unwitting, characterizes imperial Roman history as much as it does an imitative literary tradition. To complete the circle, imitation of Virgil reinforces engagement with contemporary politics inasmuch as the *Aeneid*, written in the very years that Octavian/Augustus was grappling with the definition of the *princeps* and his power, helped both to crystallize and to problematize imperial ideology.

The Latin epics (and not just the *Aeneid*) continued as central cultural and educational texts throughout the Middle Ages and Renaissance (although Silius Italicus was not disinterred until 1416). These universal poems concerned with apocalyptic struggles between good and evil might seem almost designed as models for the Christian epic poet. In the 'Alexandrian' tradition of imitation inherited by Virgil and his successors, there is no sharp demarcation between the activities of poet and critic: Ovid, Lucan and the rest are all extremely sharp and informative readers of the *Aeneid*. The same is true of post-classical epicists such as Vida, Spenser and Milton, in their readings of both Virgil and the later imperial epics. My own reading of the classical poems has been informed significantly by these 'implicit readings' of the Renaissance, an age more in sympathy than the twentieth century with imperial epic. In turn I would like to think that a sympathetic classicist's reading of the ancient poems might have something to offer modern students of their Renaissance imitators.

The following pages are a mixture of synthesis and suggestion, accompanied at every stage with close readings. In the spirit of the series I have not annotated exhaustively; my general policy has been to limit the bibliography to works of particular importance or fertility. Hercules will recognise my other thefts.

In many ways the present book is a successor to my earlier study of the *Aeneid*;[1] one of the reviewers of that work suggested that it might be deconstructed in its own terms. Whether, in conclusion, the son has been unfaithful to the father I leave it for others to judge.

The early stages of reading and thinking for this book were undertaken in the congenial surroundings of the Humanities Research Centre in Canberra during a Visiting Fellowship held in 1988. A version of part of chapter 2 was delivered as a paper to the Oxford Philological Society. I found exceptionally penetrating critical readers in my two editors (whose own writings are not the least of my debts) and in Charles Martindale. At a late stage John Henderson and David Konstan acutely confirmed my uncertainties. None of these is responsible for remaining obstinacies.

[1] Hardie (1986).

CHAPTER

I

Closure and continuation

The epic strives for totality and completion, yet is at the same time driven obsessively to repetition and reworking. From this contradiction arise the specific dynamics of the epic tradition within the general mechanisms of imitation and tradition in ancient literature; it is a contradiction that is present in a particularly acute form in Virgil's *Aeneid*, yielding a tension that energizes the epics of the first century A.D. and continues to inform such Renaissance works as Vida's *Christiad* and Milton's *Paradise Lost*.

In the case of the Homeric epics the totalizing impulse is perhaps perceived more clearly in the later Greek interpretation of the poems than in the texts as they might present themselves to an 'unbiased' modern eye. The *Iliad* and the *Odyssey* become the central cultural and educational documents of Hellenism, and interpreters both naturalistic and allegorical work hard to make of them universal poems adequate to their pre-imposed function as cultural and scientific blueprints.[1] For the committed Homerist, which is almost to say, for the committed adherent to Hellenic values, there is a text for everything in Homer if you only know how to read him. But it is already significant that two poems, rather than one, were selected as the pre-eminent monuments of the beginning of the tradition; the *Odyssey* is the successor to the *Iliad* in ways that still absorb critical debate.

The *Aeneid* is at one level a colossal exercise in definition, seeking to define the Roman epic as the new *Weltgedicht* through an act of appropriation or of literary imperialism, whereby the world of Greek culture and literature (understood as the realization of what was always potentially present in Homer) is pressed into the service of the new age in

---

[1] See Hardie (1986), ch. 1.

Rome; the poem seeks also to define the limits of that new age both in politico–historical terms and more crudely by marking out the boundaries of Roman geographical expansion as coextensive with the limits of the human and even of the natural worlds. The *Aeneid*'s claim to totality is, on the surface, far more strident than anything in the Greek tradition, and also qualitatively different in that it is pushed beyond the cultural and literary spheres into the ground of history itself. The pretensions to closure are awesome; Virgil, it is said, claimed that he was not in his right mind when he set out to write the *Aeneid*, and, if biographical play may be briefly allowed, his desire that the work be burned after his death may reflect, beyond the reported fact that three more years of polishing yet remained, a more general anxiety about the possibility of setting a *finis* to such a poem.

In its present state (and no doubt in any conceivable state of 'completion') the *Aeneid* constantly works against its own closure, remaining a text that is for ever open to new readings. I shall argue that some of the most important in that open-ended series of readings are constituted by the epics of Virgil's successors. Among twentieth-century critics, attention to the conflict between the pressure to totalize, to finalize, and the pull to leave endings open has concentrated on the political and historical aspects of the *Aeneid*'s epic 'definitions', whence the monotonously reductive debate about whether Virgil was really for or against Augustus.

There are other ways of framing the issue. Totality may be viewed either temporally or spatially. Epic's relation to time has always been problematical; as the main narrative genre it cannot escape time, and in the Homeric paradigm time is thematized in the awareness of narrator and audience that the narrative time is in a distant past, in an age other than, and different from, their own. Virgil's peculiar construction of an ideology for the present day through the narration of the legendary past attempts to forge a continuity, even identity, between the times of narrated events and narrating. This strategy of course must highlight the vast processes of change that lead from past to present; Virgil's self-imposed task, breathtakingly, is then to persuade us that with Augustus these processes are brought to a conclusion. The poetic symbol of this immobilization of history which, if successful, would indeed make of the *Aeneid* the final epic, is the Golden Age. But while the Christian epic may find ultimate rest in mankind's final return to the paradisal state from which it wandered, in Rome, where eternity is envisaged as of this world, a world identified with the 'eternal city', history has a way of taking its revenge. In mythological terms the singular achievement of Augustus is to realize a repetition of the Golden Age, that dream of primitive plenitude that was forever unattainable in the present until Virgil ran time backwards in the fourth *Eclogue*. But in the historical world of men gold tarnishes, and the first century A.D. is the history of the repeated annunciation of the return of a Golden Age whose every coming strictly speaking should be the Last Coming.[2] The difference is that between epic and romance, understanding epic as a form that strives for and attains a conclusion where all has been achieved, and romance as a form that wanders after a goal that is constantly deferred and in which each partial gain is followed only by yet another promise of that goal.[3]

In spatial terms the Virgilian and post-Virgilian epic attempts to construct a comprehensive and orderly model of the world, but it turns out that such models are inherently unstable. The instability of the Virgilian world is an open-ended invitation for succeeding epic poets to revise and redefine. In chapter 3 I examine the manifestations of this with particular reference to the charting of the locations of Heaven and Hell.

The One and the Many

Epic is a totalizing form; the agents in epic narrative are also expansive, striving for a lonely pre-eminence and ultimate omnipotence. Again the seeds are Homeric, but the full crop is reaped by Virgil and his successors. Instead of totalizing one might talk of 'maximizing': the epic hero is one who claims for himself, and for himself alone, a superlative, in Iliadic terms the accolade of 'best' (of the Achaeans), the disputed title which is the ultimate cause of the quarrel between Achilles and Agamemnon. 'Best' means, above all, 'greatest' in battle; the *aristeia*, '(deeds of) excellence', is the label attached to the typical Iliadic episode in which one of the great heroes demonstrates his prowess single-handed in battle. In the latter part of the *Iliad* Achilles who, despite his reconciliation with the Greeks, moves into a deeper isolation and self-dependence after the death of Patroclus, strains at the physical limits of the human individual as he confronts natural and divine forces. On the human level the

[2] Imperial returns of the Golden Age: Gatz (1967), 135 ff. Key passages in the epics (all reworking Virgilian topics): Lucan *Bell. Ciu.* 1.61–2; Valerius Flaccus *Argon.* 1.555–67; Silius *Pun.* 3.622–4.
[3] See Parker (1979); Quint (1989); Hardie (1992).

reappearance in battle of the individual Achilles succeeds in turning back the host of the Trojans whom the combined remainder of the Achaean captains had been unable to withstand. The *Odyssey* is not, except at the end, about martial pre-eminence, but an excellence that depends less on strength of hand leads to a parallel isolation of Odysseus, the one man who, through a combination of cunning and divine protection, escapes when all the rest of his companions perish on the journey from Troy to Ithaca. This gives to the singular number of the first word of the poem, *andra* '(the) man', an especial force. Finally, back in Ithaca Odysseus must reveal once more the overt strength of the *aristos* in the contest of the bow and the ensuing slaughter of the suitors; the prize of martial uniqueness is marital unity as Odysseus reclaims through force his right to be the sole claimant to the hand of Penelope.

Virgil's Aeneas is not isolated through the loss of all his companions, but many readers find in him a grim figure of the loneliness of power and responsibility. His is also the loneliness of the representative and original ancestor of a race; in him we meet the first clearly defined example of the 'synecdochic hero', the individual who stands for the totality of his people present and future, part for whole. The line of such heroes leads eventually to the Adam and Christ of *Paradise Lost*. Within the local narrative of the *Aeneid* the increasing hyperbole of the last books works to gain our assent to the proposition that there is a supra-individual quality to Aeneas (and Turnus);[4] the adequacy of one to all is summed up in the description of Aeneas' shield (itself a microcosmic icon) as (8.447–8) 'one against all the weapons of the Latins' *unum omnia contra|tela Latinorum*. This is the Achillean side of Aeneas; the Odyssean theme of the one survivor is inverted in the fate of Palinurus, the one man who dies that many may survive as Neptune demands (5.814–15): 'There will be just one whom you will miss, lost at sea; one life will be given for many' *unus erit tantum amissum quem gurgite quaeres;|unum pro multis dabitur caput.*[5]

Within the *Aeneid* the lengthiest essay in the definition of the Roman hero is found in the Speech of Anchises in book 6; his review of the souls of unborn Romans ends with an apostrophe of Fabius Maximus Cunctator, who is characterized both by superlativeness and by singularity, 6.845–6 'you are the one called "Greatest", the one man who by

---

[4] Hardie (1986), 285–91; index s.vv. 'royal metaphor' (a phrase of Northrop Frye's). Cf. also Williams (1978), 199–205 on 'the theme of one man in single combat against a whole army' in Latin epic. [5] See pp. 32–3 below.

delaying restores to us the state' *tu* Maximus *ille es,|*unus *qui nobis cunctando restituis rem.* By name he is 'the greatest', and as such suited to be the one man who single-handed preserved the state. Line 846 is famous as a quotation of Ennius;[6] this ending to a parade that centres on Augustus ('this, this is the man' *hic uir, hic est* 6.791) seeks to justify by precedent the place within the Roman state of a supreme individual, an *unus homo*, by reference to one of the staunchest upholders of Republican values. It was of course Augustus' claim in 27 B.C. to 'restore the republic' (*restituere rem publicam*). At *Fasti* 1.587–616, on 13 January, the anniversary of the 'restoration of the Republic', Ovid brings Fabius Maximus and Augustus into close association, in an evaluation of the name 'Augustus' bestowed on Octavian on that day: Pompey's cognomen *Magnus* ('The Great') reflected the greatness of his deeds, but 'greater' (*maior*) was the name of his conqueror (Julius Caesar); *Maximus*, the cognomen of Fabius, is the 'greatest' possible name – in terms of human honours, but *Augustus* outdoes *Maximus* since it is a sacred name. One of the etymologies offered by Ovid is from *augere* 'make to increase'. 'Greatest' marks a limit in size, but the expansiveness of the name 'Augustus' is freed from the rules of grammatical degree.[7]

National salvation ensured by the extension over the whole state of the family head's *patria potestas* justifies the synecdochic hero in Virgil. Ovid explores elsewhere the implications of the absorption of the state into the body of one individual. He plays further games with Fabian numbers in the narrative of the Fabii at the Cremera at *Fasti* 2.193–242: *one* day that saw the death of 306 members of the *gens Fabia, one* family that alone provided the strength of the whole state, a troop of privates any *one* of whom was suited to be the general (2.195–200). The episode, like Anchises' review of heroes, ends with a near-quotation of the Ennian line on the Cunctator, but with a twist (2.239–42): 'For there was one survivor of the Fabian family, a boy below age and not yet able to bear arms, left behind so that in the future you, Maximus, could be born, in order to restore the state by delaying'

> nam puer impubes et adhuc non utilis armis
> *unus* de Fabia gente relictus erat,
> scilicet ut posses olim tu, Maxime, nasci,
> cui res cunctando restituenda foret.

[6] *unus homo nobis cunctando restituit rem, Ann.* 363 Skutsch.
[7] On the play with degrees of *magnus* in Virgil, see Feeney (1986b), 12–13, 24 n. 90.

The key word *unus* is displaced from the great Cunctator on to the single under-age survivor of the *gens* in 477 B.C.: singular greatness is precariously dependent on a single line of descent. This is Ovid's comment on the coda to the Speech of Anchises, the lament for the imperial successor Marcellus, the youth who did not survive.[8]

In the *Metamorphoses* Ovid gears up for the imperial (and poetic) expansionism of the last book by tilting another innocent Ennian quotation in the direction of the *princeps*, as Mars reminds Jupiter of what he had promised in that earlier epic (14.814): 'there will be one whom you will elevate to the blue sky' *unus erit quem tu tolles in caerula caeli/templa* (cf. Ennius *Ann.* 54–5 Skutsch). Romulus' reward is now due since (808–9): 'The Roman state is firm on its great foundation and its security hangs on *one* ruler',[9] words which could refer as well to the first *princeps* as to the first king. The singularity of Romulus here stands in relation to duality as well as to the totality of the Roman state. Ennius' emphatic *unus* probably marked in the first place a contrast to the *other* twin, Remus, fated to die. Ovid twists Ennius again by indicating that Romulus' sole rule emerges also from the previous sharing of kingship with the Sabine Titus Tatius (805–6: for the Romans a shared throne is proverbially unstable); this co-regency was the diplomatic solution to the war between Romans and Sabines, whose confrontation, like the quarrel between Romulus and Remus, was one of the events in early Roman history that prefigured the civil wars of the late Republic. In the last book of the *Metamorphoses* Ovid returns to veiled comment on the *unus homo* in the story of Cipus who thoughtfully warns the Roman people that the miraculous horns that he has sprouted mark him out as king of Rome (15.594–5): 'He said "There is here one man who, unless you cast him out of the city, will be king."' Cipus averts from himself and his fellow-citizens the danger of his becoming king by turning himself into a scapegoat, an Oedipus rather than a Romulus.[10]

---

[8] The 'continuity theme' in this episode and other aspects of the parallel between the *gens Fabia* and the imperial dynasty are excellently discussed by Harries (1991). The numerical conceits are already present in Ovid's source, Livy 2.49; Livy also extends Fabian 'uniqueness' to the K. Fabius in command of an army against Veii in 481 B.C. (2.43.6) 'Fabius had rather more trouble with his citizens than with the enemy. That one man, the consul himself, upheld the state (*unus ille uir, ipse consul, rem publicam sustinuit*), which the army out of hatred of the consul did its best to undermine' (note the context of civil discord). On Marcellus, see p. 92 below.

[9] At line 809 I read *et* rather then *nec*, for the reasons sketched out above.

[10] See Feeney (1991) for discussion of the way in which Ovid's treatment of Julius

6

In the imperial epic of the later first century A.D. (as in the historical empire) the 'one man' remains a problem, most starkly in Lucan where the Republic is destroyed by the struggle between Caesar and Pompey to become that one man. The 'maximizing' hero and the 'totalizing' historical stage collide in the paradox of 1.110–11: 'Rome's greatness, which owned the sea, the earth, the whole world, was not big enough for two men.' Pompey has as cognomen *Magnus*; this is the occasion for a wide-ranging play on the adjective and its comparative and superlative degrees *maior, maximus* that places the nature of Pompey's heroism within the epic's generic obligation to be 'big, great' ('greater' than its predecessors, even 'greatest').[11] The *Bellum Ciuile* is a superb study in the way that the illusions of power turn into reality, in what one might call the danger of the representative principle.[12] Individual leaders become many-handed monsters because of the obedience of a mass of other individuals. Lucan, following Livy and Ovid, plays with the opposition or coincidence of 'general' *dux* and 'soldier' *miles*. In the mutiny in *Bellum Ciuile* 5 Caesar is abruptly reminded of the fiction on which his power rests (5.252–4): 'Lopped of so many hands and left with almost nothing but his own sword, the man who dragged so many nations into war realised that drawn swords belong not to the general but to the soldier.' Conversely in the desert march of book 9 Cato paradoxically becomes a true *dux* by making himself a *miles*, voluntarily sharing all the privations of his troops (9.401–2).[13] It is the individual Pompey who is decapitated, but this is equated with the loss of Rome itself as 'head of the world' *caput mundi* (9.123–5). The final standard of Pompey's heroism is his ability to abdicate his political representative status; it is weakness that leads him to abandon control of his cause by yielding to Cicero's rhetoric before Pharsalia, but it is (a passing moment of) strength when later (7.659–64) he attempts to offer himself as a substitute victim for Rome, diverting the gods' wrath from the state to that other supra-individual entity of which he is the head, his own family.[14] It is of course not Pompey but Caesar who becomes, by the traditional epic standards of military and political power, 'greatest', 'the one man', the imperial Everyman without whom there is no independent action; this is expressed

Caesar and Augustus in the *Metamorphoses* reveals 'the appropriation of the corporate by the individual' (213).

[11] Feeney (1986a).

[12] On this, and much else of relevance, see Henderson (1988).

[13] See also 7.87–8; 7.250–4.   [14] See pp. 54–6 below.

in the sudden withering of the traditional organs of state into the one body of Caesar on his entry into Rome (3.105–9): 'The consuls did not sit radiant in their hallowed seats, nor were the praetors, constitutionally second in power, present, and the curule seats were empty. Caesar was everything (*omnia Caesar erat*); the senate was present as witness to the voice of a private man.'[15] Much of the hyperbole of the *Bellum Ciuile* is based on the 'one against all' or 'one for many' principle; the supreme emblem of this is the *aristeia* of the Caesarian Scaeva in book 6 who single-handedly fights off a Pompeian army (6.140–2): 'A position that could not successfully be taken with a thousand squadrons nor by Caesar in full force, was snatched from the victors by one man' *quem non mille simul turmis nec Caesare* toto|*auferret Fortuna locum uictoribus* unus|*eripuit*. Here the *totus/unus* contrast is heightened by the paradoxical application of the epithet of totality to an individual; when Caesar is already *omnia* then the superior power of the *unus* Scaeva is indeed terrible.

In the *Thebaid* of Statius emphasis is shifted away further (in comparison with Lucan) from singular pre-eminence to the paradoxes and confusions of duality. Neither Polynices nor Eteocles succeeds in realising a Caesarian or Catonian uniqueness, but, to an extent, the secondary character Tydeus becomes the repository for the *unus/omnes* conceits of the earlier Latin epic tradition, both in his single-handed massacre of the Theban ambush at the end of book 2 and in his *aristeia* in book 8. At the orgiastic climax of incestuously doubling violence in book 11 Statius uses the language of the one and the many in what amounts to a condemnation of epic's power to memorialize singular events (11.577–9): 'In all lands and for all time may one day alone witness this crime; may this infamous prodigy fall from the memory of posterity, and kings alone recall this battle'

> *omnibus* in terris scelus hoc *omni*que sub aeuo
> uiderit *una* dies, monstrumque infame futuris
> excidat, et *soli* memorent haec proelia reges.

In Silius' *Punica* the rhetoric of one and many, of great, greater and

---

[15] Epic hyperbole finds an echo in Seneca's advice to a prince, *De Clementia* 1.5.1 'you are the soul of your state, it is your body', quoted by Kantorowicz (1957), 215 n. 65. In a suggestive 'Epilogue' Kantorowicz raises, without fully answering, the question of how far medieval 'corporationist' theories of the prince in which the state is viewed as 'the supra-individual collective body of the Prince' (218) are indebted to antique models.

greatest, is brought back into line with Republican values. In book 6 Regulus is established as a paradigm for Republican 'greatness', the 'greater' the more ready he is to sacrifice, or 'devote', himself for the public good.[16] His name itself is perhaps significant, 'little king', the greatest Roman hero of his day but who presents the least risk of aiming at sole rule. The model of Regulus is immediately imitated by Fabius Cunctator: Silius runs through the *unus/omnes* theme at the beginning of book 7, firstly in his own proem to Fabius' exploits, and secondly in Cilnius' narration to Hannibal of the story of the 300 Fabii. The book starts with reworkings of the Ennian, Virgilian and Ovidian models (7.1–8): 'Meanwhile Fabius was the sole hope in the state of panic . . . His mind greater than human took no account of spears, swords and war horses; against so many thousands of Carthaginians and their invincible leader, against so many armies he went forth alone, and in himself he embodied all the arms and men of Italy:'

> interea trepidis Fabius spes *unica* rebus . . .
> sed mens humana *maior* non tela nec enses   (5)
> nec fortes spectabat equos: tot milia contra
> Poenorum inuictumque ducem, tot in agmina *solus*
> ibat et in sese *cuncta*[17] arma uirosque gerebat.

In *arma uirosque*, with its allusion to the first words of the *Aeneid*, we see a hero who embodies whole epics (outbidding the *Aeneid*'s 'arms and the (singular) man'). The comparative *maior* both reminds us of Regulus' magnification and points to the superlative *Maximus* that is in every sense Fabius' proper name. But this singularly great hero has as his goal the curbing of excess through the defeat of Hannibal, whose epic (Caesarian) pretensions he deflates through the imposition of 'limit' *modus* (7.12) and an 'end' *finis* (13) by his own control, *moderamen* (15). As the true Republican hero Fabius has the virtue of his ancestor Hercules but none of the tendency to transgressive excess – unlike Hannibal who is soon seen in one of his most expansive moods, boasting of the flight to the ends of the earth of the Roman generals and wielding an Achillean shield emblazoned with a representation of the whole universe (7.96–122). The prisoner Cilnius who tells Hannibal about Fabius plays the numbers game with the story of the 300 Fabii and the war with Veii: three hundred whose expansive *uirtus* did not allow the

---

[16] *maior, maius: Pun.* 6.416, 426, 533. On *deuotio* see pp. 28–9 below.

[17] In line 10 we have the Ennian and Virgilian *cunctando; cuncta* in line 8 looks like a tease. Silius suggests a pun in Ennius' and Virgil's *unus . . . cuncta-ndo.*

enemy the chance to make a full tally of the number of the *uiri*, each one of whom was 'second to none in their courage' (7.55). But Fabius Maximus alone is more than a replacement for those three hundred who were more than three hundred (63–4).

One and Two[18]

The totalizing or maximizing tendency of the epic is always threatened by the possibility of division within the totality or of rivalry for the superlative. The *Iliad* tells what happens when the authority of the supreme commander of the Achaeans is challenged by a second claimant to the title of 'best'. The epic power struggle constantly throws up doubles; the Latin epic greatly extends this innate tendency of the genre, because of the dualities that structure political power and its dissolution at Rome. The founding myth of the city, of the principate and of civil war is the Romulus and Remus story: Rome arises out of the violent replacement of a twosome by a unique founder.[19] With the expulsion of the last Tarquin, monarchy is replaced by the dyarchy of the consuls, not always a perfectly harmonious twosome (consular discord is a particular theme of Silius); the increasing tensions within the Republican consular system lead eventually to the submersion of dyarchy in the uncontrolled divisions of civil war, which in turn are patched over by another monarchical regime, although Augustus will maintain the Republican consular dyarchy as a constitutional fiction. Brothers, harmonious or discordant, continue to be a theme in the history of the first-century imperial household: Tiberius and Drusus, Gaius and Lucius, Nero and Britannicus,[20] Titus and Domitian.

In the next chapter I examine the phenomenon of the epic double with the help of a particular theory of the origins and function of sacrifice, that of René Girard; here an example will suffice from the divided world of Lucan's *Bellum Ciuile*.[21] Here civil war cleaves apart a Roman state

[18] For parallel phenomena in later epic (doubtless to an extent a reflection of the classical models here discussed), see Fowler (1964), 7 ff., ch. 2; Shoaf (1985).

[19] For speculation on connections between the Romulus and Remus story and the dual organization of early Rome, see Cornell (1975), 29–31. See also Alföldi (1974), ch. 6 'Zweiteilung und Doppelmonarchie'.

[20] Tac. *Ann.*13.17 (men at the funeral of Britannicus) 'thinking of the discord of brothers in ancient times and the impossibility of a partnership on the throne'.

[21] Masters' seminal work (1992) is the first to reveal fully the extent of the play of duality and doubles in Lucan. The gladiatorial pair, a dominant image in Lucan, functions as another parody of the consular duality. On division and duality in Statius, see now the dazzling essay by Henderson (1991).

which is on the point of becoming a true cosmopolis, a unified world-state, through the success of Roman arms against outside enemies; Roman *uir-tus* is as expansive as the epic *uir*. The *concordia* that should be the mark of the constitutional division of supreme power between the two consuls turns to *discordia* when the two supreme men (now not as consuls but as a parodic imitation of that institution created when the third member of the triumvirate, Crassus, is killed) agree to disagree and to contend for sole power, monarchy. But even as Caesar succeeds in wresting that power to himself, and as Pompey fades away, another version of the duality is established, in the opposition of the figures of Caesar and Cato, or of the Principate and the Republic. One of the distorting effects of the power struggle is to turn the representative of the free Republic into a parody of the tyrannical Caesar as Cato becomes another *unus homo*. In book 2 Cato would see his representativeness as that of Palinurus, the individual sacrificed for the common good.[22] But there is something megalomaniac in Cato's altruism; on his march through the desert in book 9 he tries to live up to an Aeneas' protective concern for his men, but the narrative is taken up with a catalogue of deaths of members of the rank and file, as vulnerable as the companions of Odysseus. Eventually, after the present ending of the poem, Cato will die as literally the 'one man', as the last Republican, the sole survivor of his race.[23] What will be left will be Caesar – everything but nothing, the living corpse of Rome.

The continuation of epic

Imperial Latin epic takes to an extreme the innate tendency of the genre to the expansive and the comprehensive; yet it does not escape from the contrary pulls towards continuation and repetition that deny to even the most arrogantly hyperbolical epic the possibility of making a final and all-inclusive statement.

Homeric epic in its oral phase exists only through the possibility of reworking at each new performance. The monumental fixation of the *Iliad* and the *Odyssey* perpetuates large and unified structures which are nevertheless still subject to the quality shared with the shorter recitations presumably typical of the main oral phase, of being parts of a larger whole, the entire time-span of the legendary and historical actions of men

[22] See pp. 32–3 below.
[23] Ahl, Davis, Pomeroy (1986), 2502 for Rome reduced *again* to one man in Lucan's Cato, as originally in Virgil's Aeneas.

and gods; ἔνθεν ἑλών is the phrase that describes how the epic poet 'picks up' the story at a particular point (*Od.* 8.500), to end at a point where he or another may resume in the future. 'For practical reasons, and also in keeping with its own deliberate style, the art form is always calculated for continuation; it does not aim at formal conclusions in which its movement comes to a stop.'[24] The two Homeric epics are part of the epic cycle, which is to say that they both continue and will be continued by other narratives; this is very clear in the alternative two lines at the end of the *Iliad*, 'so they busied themselves with the funeral of Hector, and there came an Amazon, daughter of great-hearted man-slaying Ares', where the arrival of Penthesilea introduces the next epic, the *Aithiopis*. From the point of view of certain ancient scholars, the *Odyssey* already continues itself, for Aristophanes and Aristarchus are reported to have said that the end of the poem is to be located at 23.296.

Virgil's choice of epic subject-matter transforms the role of continuation. The *Aeneid* may be thought of as the first epic in a new, Roman, epic cycle, the final work in which would be the *Augustiad* that Virgil chose not to write. The full cycle, if realized, would be a series of epics that together covered the same span as the single-epic *Annals* of Ennius, from the Fall of Troy down to the poet's own day. In a sense, of course, the cycle is already realized within the *Aeneid* because of the peculiar way in which the narrative of Aeneas manages by various devices to narrate simultaneously the whole of the future history of the descendants of Aeneas. After the *Aeneid* epics on Roman historical subjects inevitably read as a part of that cycle defined by Virgil, either working with or against the predominant features of the Virgilian outline; the former in the case of Silius' *Punica*, the latter in the case of Lucan's *Bellum Ciuile*. Insofar as the *Aeneid* performs in other ways the all-inclusive function of the *Annals* of Ennius, it reasserts its quality as a totalizing epic; but it also manages to leave itself open to continuation. This is partly the achievement of the end of the poem, which as so many have felt is not an ending at all (except for Turnus), merely the beginning of the history of the Aeneadae once they have vindicated their right to settle in the land of the future Rome. The end is also a beginning in another sense, in that the final picture of Aeneas hot in anger is scarcely to be distinguished from the Aeneas hot in anger who first leaps into his own narrative on the night of the Sack of Troy in book 2 – or from the incensed Juno who launches

[24] Fränkel (1975), 14.

the action *in medias res* at the beginning of the first book. This ring-composition is a structural imitation of features in the *Iliad* and the *Odyssey*, but executed in such a way as both to affirm and frustrate our sense of an ending.

The classic example of an epic ending that is a beginning is the close of *Paradise Lost*, that starts the 'heroes' off on the epic journey of mankind from paradise lost to paradise regained as Adam and Eve 'Through Eden took their solitary way'. At this point, *after* a poem that has, in Marvell's words, comprehended 'Heaven, hell, earth, chaos, all', and whose various actors have approached a synecdochic or representative totality, we are left with a pair of individuals, now truly alone until the final reintegration of the human race through redemption, and for whom 'The world was all *before* them'. The self-conscious play on beginnings and endings had been taken up with gusto by the ancient imitators of Virgil. Ovid introduces the *last* book of the *Metamorphoses* with the long Speech of Pythagoras that reworks the Speech of Homer with which Ennius introduces the *first* book of his epic. Here the gesture is primarily one of closure: Ovid's 'epic' makes a bid to be the final and most comprehensive in the line of epics inaugurated by Ennius; but within Ovid's own œuvre the *Metamorphoses* will be continued by the *Fasti*, the poem on the Roman calendar whose theme is defined by one of the senses of 'my times' *mea tempora* in the prologue of the *Metamorphoses* (1.4), and whose first Roman festival is that of Aesculapius, the god whose introduction to Rome comes almost at the end of the *Metamorphoses*. The linear narrative thrust of the *Metamorphoses* will henceforth be transformed into the cyclical recurrence of the imperial Roman year.[25]

In the final book of Silius' *Punica* Hannibal sails from Italy to Africa, but as Italy disappears over the horizon he has second thoughts, and turns his ships in their course. This is an attempt to steer the epic narrative back to the renewal of war in Italy; there ensues a replay of the storm which begins the *Aeneid*, and which had also driven Virgil's hero from his course to Italy. But where Aeneas' consequent landing in an alien Africa had marked the beginning of a new series of wanderings whose final goal would be the foundation of Rome, Hannibal's landing in his home country completes the preconditions for Scipio's final and total defeat of Carthage. As with the *Metamorphoses* Silius' concluding return to a beginning strongly asserts the conclusion of unfinished

---

[25] Barchiesi (1991), 6; Hardie (1991c) on beginnings and ends in the Janus episode.

business, the conflict between Rome and Carthage, the thought of which drives Juno into action at the beginning of the *Aeneid*; but insofar as that conflict is but a stage in the longer history to which the *Aeneid* alludes, we are also reminded that the triumph of Scipio Africanus that comes at the very end of the epic is not in fact the end of the story.[26] Statius also alludes to the inaugural storm of the *Aeneid* just before the ending of the *Thebaid* in the simile at 12.650–5 comparing the onrush of Theseus against Thebes to the unleashing of the storm winds from Aeolus' kingdom. Here however the violence of the storm is controlled by Jupiter, not Juno, and allusion to *Aeneid* 1 is combined with allusion to the final spearthrow of Aeneas in book 12, like a thunderbolt.[27] Closure is emphatic, but at the same time Statius raises once more the question, perhaps left unanswered at the end of the *Aeneid*, of the possibility of distinguishing between just and unjust violence. At the very end of the *Thebaid* Statius speaks of the approach of a new poetic *furor* to fill the sails of an epic performance of the lamentations for the dead heroes, deliberately fostering the impression that this is a to some extent arbitrary suspension of a poem that could be continued (as at 1.15–7 Statius had indicated his excision of a plot for his epic from a Theban history extending far back into the past).[28] Looking beyond those funerals we may also glimpse the return of the Epigoni.

Repetition

As a product of the oral tradition epic has a set towards continuation; from these origins it also carries with it the habit of repetition, the repetition of verbal formulas, scenes, themes and structures. The nature and function of Homeric repetition has been at the centre of modern analysis and criticism: repetition drained of significance because its sole purpose is to ensure the smooth running of an oral 'machine' with its standardized parts or repetition charged with the meaning of literary pattern or even of ritual? For the imitators of Homer the question

---

[26] Conversely Silius gives us a version of the *final* duel between Aeneas and Turnus in the encounter of Hannibal and the Saguntine Murrus that forms the climax of the fighting in the *first* book of the *Punica*, 1.456–517.

[27] On 'combinatorial allusion', see Hardie (1990b).

[28] On the ending of the *Thebaid*, see also pp. 46–8 below.

becomes one of how to accommodate repetition as a mark of the genre with the self-consciousness of the completely literary artist.

Virgil makes a virtue of necessity, taking repetition (though not so much on the verbal level) to an extreme in the *Aeneid*. Meaning here is largely generated through the repetition of situations and actions; as the actors move through space and time they seem condemned to relive the experiences of their pasts.

The function of repetition within the *Aeneid* has been illuminatingly discussed by David Quint in an essay that distinguishes between two forms of repetition, 'regressive repetition' as 'obsessive circular return to a traumatic past', and 'repetition-as-reversal' that allows an element of difference by which that past is mastered.[29] Quint well shows how the dominant thrust of the last half of the epic towards a conclusive repetition through inversion of the earlier defeat of the Trojans is complicated by the suggestion in the last scene of the possibility of an indefinite cycle of retaliatory revenge.[30] We have already looked at ways in which the *Aeneid* points more openly to repetitions outside the strict chronological limits of the story of Aeneas; the developing repetitions within the plot proper thus define the poem as a segment of a series . . . Augustus. A number of critics have seen here an analogy with the repetitiousness of Biblical typology, an analogy that only holds if Augustus really can be all in all.

The impossibility of circumscribing repetition *within* the *Aeneid* overflows into the 'repetitions' of the poem in the works of the successors of Virgil. This reference outside of the poem also allows for the possibility of other epics to 'complete' or rewrite the *Aeneid*, extending the compulsion of characters (and the poet himself) in the *Aeneid* to re-enact and rewrite the past, their own or others'.

In the *Aeneid* repetition is above all of Troy and events at Troy. War in Italy is, as the Sibyl indicates, a repetition of the Trojan War (6.88–90); it is also the consummation of the Roman epic poet's powers, a 'greater

---

[29] Quint (1991). For this twofold typology of repetition Quint is indebted to Brooks (1985), who in turn draws on Freudian models of repetition. See also Shoaf (1985), 14 ff. distinguishing between 'repetition' (allowing for freedom and originality) and 'reiteration' (sterile return) in *Paradise Lost*; related analyses in Schwartz (1988). For a more pessimistic view of repetition in Statius' *Thebaid* as an 'anti-structure of regression', the product of guilt and revenge, see Henderson (1991), 41.

[30] Quint here has the analyses of Girard in mind, on which see further ch. 2.

work' *maius opus* (7.45). In the first half of the poem the most extended repetition of Troy is encountered in the city of Buthrotum, the home of Helenus and Andromache. This place is a monument to what was, as exact a replica as possible of the vanished Troy. Helenus, the king, is a prophet and provides Aeneas with a large part of what he needs to know about the future, but his wife Andromache lives exclusively in the past, in perpetual attendance on the cenotaph of her first husband Hector. Quint sees Buthrotum as the example *par excellence* of regressive repetition, a lifeless imitation; on seeing Aeneas Andromache is unable to decide whether *he* is alive or a dead *simulacrum*, sharing the confusion of Aeneas before the apparition of Andromache's husband Hector at 2.281–6. *That* vision however was charged with the fullness of political and poetic transmission to the future (see pp. 102–3 below). Allusion to *Odyssey* 11 reinforces the sense that Buthrotum is a place of the dead, a landscape indeterminate as to its location in the upper or lower worlds (on such confusion see chapter 3). Unlike the war in Italy, this reworking of Homeric places is very much a 'lesser work' *minus opus*; if we are introduced to Buthrotum with the 'unbelievable rumour' *incredibilis fama* that Helenus has succeeded in the task imposed on Aeneas of transferring a Trojan kingdom overseas and even of ruling in a Greek land, nevertheless the 'lofty city' of Buthrotum (3.293) turns out to be a pale shadow of the original: (349–51) 'on I go and I recognise a *small* Troy, an imitation of the *great* Pergamon, and a dried-up stream bearing the name of Xanthus'. Andromache has regressed from union with the conqueror Neoptolemus to a second marriage with a Trojan (297), and in a sense is still married to her first, dead, husband. Fulfilment for her would be the condition of the dead Dido, a shade reunited with the shade of her former husband at 6.473–4. Aeneas by contrast is doomed to obey the command of the 'shadow' of his first wife Creusa to leave the Inferno of Troy sacked and to take a foreign wife from the land that will be his new home (2.771–94).

In this place of memory Andromache stands as a warning by the poet to himself of the danger of epic failure: she looks to Ascanius to re-embody the 'former virtue' of Troy, roused by the thought of father Aeneas and uncle Hector, pointing to the continuity of generational succession,[31] but her own devotion to the memory of Hector involves

---

[31] See pp. 91–2 below.

calling on the shades of a tomb empty even of a body.[32] Memory here is inert, limited to shadowy imitations that will never take on life and expand as the successful epic must. In his parting words at 3.493 ff. Aeneas combines the topics of fare-well (*uiuite felices*) with the language of the funerary epitaph. He envies his hosts 'the story of whose fortunes has now been brought to a conclusion', and comments wearily on the indefinite series of adventures that confronts his own followers (494): 'We are called from one set of adventures to another' *nos alia ex aliis in fata uocamur* – but in truth it is the word 'other' *alius* that contains the promise of a new and different future. He hopes that this Troy has been made with *better* omens than the old and that it is *less* exposed to Greek attack – comparatives, but not of *magnus*.

This episode about imitations is itself one of the Virgilian passages imitated by Lucan in the visit by Caesar to the site of Troy in *Bellum Ciuile* 9.961–79. Caesar unwittingly steps across the trickle in the dust that was once the raging river Xanthus (974–5). Lucan immediately makes explicit what in Virgil had been implicit, namely the connection between geographical relic and the power of the epic poet to replicate (and magnify) in the promise at 980–6 to bestow eternal life on the 'hero' of his epic. The irony is that Caesar, greatest of the great epic heroes, will succeed only in reproducing in Rome and Italy the diminution virtually to extinction that is the state of the present-day Troy.[33]

Alius, the word repeated in Aeneas' *nos alia ex aliis in fata uocamur*, is one of a number of words of iteration, *alius, alter, iterum, rursus*, etc. whose occurrence in epic is always worth attention. *Alius* can mean both old and new, another of the same or a different other; and that is precisely the issue, a matter for historical and literary judgment. *Alius* and *alter* prove slippery words in two pivotal attempts in the *Aeneid* to control the future through an appeal to the past, firstly by the Sibyl at 6.89: 'Another (*alius*) Achilles has already been born in Latium'; and secondly in Juno's attempt at 7.321–2 to define events in Italy as a second Trojan War: 'Venus' offspring is just the same as Hecuba's, a second (*alter*) Paris, and again (*iterum*) funeral torches light up the restored Troy.'[34] The quality of

---

[32] See pp. 40–8 below on 're-embodiment'; pp. 61, 64–5 on the empowering of epic from the tomb.

[33] See pp. 106–7 below.

[34] Other instances of *iterum:* e.g. *Aen.* 6.93–4; Luc. *Bell. Ciu.* 1.692; Stat. *Theb.* 7.159, 11.329, 12.690.

17

the 'otherness' of the epic poet in relation to his predecessors is equally crucial (and contested): Horace quotes a critics' definition of Ennius by reference both to the typical virtues of the epic heroes of whom he sings and to the epic poet that he hopes to succeed, at *Epistles* 2.1.50: 'Ennius, both wise and brave, and a second Homer (*alter Homerus*).' It will be left for the Christian epic to make of *alius* an unambivalent marker of the progression from an imperfect to a perfect state: in Vida's *Christiad* the Virgilian *alius* denotes the transition from the Age of the Law to the Age of Grace, from the material to the spiritual.[35]

---

[35] See Hardie 1993a.

Sacrifice and substitution

Sacrificial crisis in the epic

The *Aeneid* begins and ends with sacrifice. In terms of absolute chronology the main narrative starts in book 2 with the dilemma presented to the Trojans by the Wooden Horse ('an offering' to Minerva, *Aen.* 2.31),[1] a dilemma resolved by the words of a Greek, Sinon, who claims to have escaped the fate of human sacrifice, and by the suffering of a Trojan, Laocoon, who, in the act of sacrificing a bull, is himself, together with his sons, cast into the role of a human victim at his own altar. The last action of the epic is another human sacrifice: as Aeneas plunges his sword into Turnus' breast he cries out (12.948–9) 'It is Pallas, Pallas who *sacrifices* (*immolat*) you with this wound'.[2] Other ways of reckoning beginning and end also bring us up against sacrifice: Juno's first speech, launching us *in medias res*, ends with the bellicose goddess' anxiety that unless she avenges herself men will no longer pay her altars the honour of sacrifice (1.48–9). The paradigm of Oilean Ajax, to which she appeals, inverts the motif of the scapegoat, 'one for all' *unus pro omnibus* (the Palinurus model), as Juno recalls the destruction by Minerva of the *whole* Greek fleet and its men 'because of the crime of *one*

---

[1] On the possible origin of the story of the Trojan Horse in scapegoat ritual, see Burkert (1979), 61–2.

[2] The 'sacrifice' of Turnus stands in for the narrative of the sacrifice of the eight victims who are taken prisoner by Aeneas at 10.517–20, led in the funeral procession of Pallas at 11.81–2, but whose killing is never actually described, unlike the human victims captured and sacrificed by Achilles as 'blood-payment for Patroclus', *Iliad* 21.27–32, 23.175–6 (with *Il.* 21.28 ποινὴν Πατρόκλοιο 'the penalty for the death of Patroclus', cf. *Aen.* 12.949 *poenam scelerato ex sanguine sumit* '[Pallas] exacts the penalty from your criminal blood').

man' (1.41). The furthest forward limit of epic prophecy, the triumph of
Augustus on the Shield of Aeneas, confirms the *pax deorum* with the
sacrifice of bullocks at all the temples of Rome (8.719). Sacrifice at the
end of Roman history as represented on the Shield echoes sacrifice at the
beginning, in the reconciliation of Roman and Sabine (8.639–41).[3]

The ending of civil war between Octavian and Antony is formally
marked by the sacrificial institutions of the Roman state; the resolution
of the quarrel between Aeneas and Turnus, a first version of that final
civil war, *should* have been regulated by one of the most elaborate scenes
of sacrificial ritual in the *Aeneid*, the *foedus* between Aeneas and Latinus
described at 12.161–215. But violence erupts once more to frustrate the
terms of the treaty; the sacred fires of the altars become the torches of war
(12.283–301). At 296 Messapus savagely comments on the replacement
of animal with human victims as he kills Aulestes: 'He's got it. This is a
better victim to offer the great gods' *hoc habet, haec melior magnis data
victima diuis* (note here also the gladiatorial phrase *hoc habet*). This, the
first deliberate confrontation in the battle, is balanced by the last, that of
Aeneas and Turnus: both are 'sacrificial'.[4] It is only through the
unbridled riot of discord and anger (12.313–14) that Aeneas and Turnus
finally meet in a very different version of the duel envisaged by the terms
of the treaty. In Aeneas' final outburst of violence and anger the
institutionally sanctioned sacrifice of animals is replaced with (sub-
stituted by) the more powerful sacrifice of a man. *Finis.*

Within *Aeneid* 12 we are shown the violence that results from the
breakdown of an established sacrificial order, leading to a chaos that is

---

[3] The war between Romans and Sabines and its resolution are the first properly
historical scenes on the Shield; the scene of the twins and the wolf is precultural,
preverbal. Sacrificial framing is already present in the *Georgics:* the sacrifices of state
religion before the poetic temple at the beginning of book 3 are answered by the
bugonia at the end of book 4, a sacrifice that provides an alternative to the expiation
of Trojan crime with Roman blood that Virgil complains of at the end of book 1.
[4] With *melior* cf. the inverse substitution at 5.483 ('a better life instead of Dares'
death' *meliorem animam pro morte Daretis*), on which see p. 52 below. This is one of
the several links between books 12 and 5, where the sacrificial framing of the games
also turns into uncontrolled violence as the Trojan women snatch fire from the
altars of Neptune, 5.661 (cf. 12.283). On these links and other aspects of the theme of
sacrifice, see Putnam (1965), ch. 2. At 12.301 the *nidor* given off by the beard of
Ebysus, set alight with a torch from the altar, translates κνῖσα 'smell of burnt
sacrifices'. One may also reflect on the connections of *hostis, hostia, hostire,
hostimentum* in ancient etymologizing: see Maltby (1991), s.vv.

only resolved through the 'victimization' of one of the parties to that violence. We have, in other words, an almost too neatly schematic dramatization of René Girard's theory of the 'sacrificial crisis', the term with which Girard characterizes the breakdown of the social and cultural order, to be resolved only through a repetition of the primitive direction of the community's reserve of violence onto a surrogate victim, an act that Girard sees at the basis of institutional sacrificial practice and of the cultural order itself.[5] 'The disappearance of the sacrificial rites coincides with the disappearance of the difference between impure violence and purifying violence . . . The sacrificial distinction . . . cannot be obliterated without obliterating all other differences as well' (p. 49). For Girard the accepted practices of sacrifice, 'beneficial violence', are a mask for the harmful violence that without sacrifice would rage uncontrolled (p. 37). The killing of Turnus is the act on which the Roman cultural order is founded; Virgil narrates a senseless vengeance-killing which is masked, in the words of the killer, as a sacrifice, but whose true nature many readers experience as quite other. As 'sacrifice' the death of Turnus represents a reimposition of order; but as uncontrolled rage, revenge pure and simple rather than the judicial retribution envisaged by the terms of the treaty, it retains its potential to repeat itself in fresh outbursts of chaotic anger (the dreary catalogue of vengeance-killings of Roman civil war).

Aeneas' role as sacrificant has a much wider significance; as ritual operator on behalf of his people he prefigures the sacrificial role of the *princeps*, an equation made in visual form on the Ara Pacis where the figure of Augustus, head veiled, advances on the south side; if he rounded the corner he would enter the world of legend and merge with his double in the shape of Aeneas, represented in a similar pose and engaged in the sacrifice of the Alban sow to the Penates. In the *Aeneid* Aeneas marks the entry of his people into the promised land of Italy with the sacrifice on the first sighting at 3.543–7, the ritual feast of emmer wheat cakes at 7.107–29 and the sacrifice of the sow at 8.81–4. Thus it is grimly appropriate that

---

[5] Girard (1977). Girard's analysis is developed largely through an interpretation of Greek tragedy, and has in turn fed back fruitfully into the criticism of tragedy, in e.g. Zeitlin (1982); Foley (1985) (useful survey of the area in ch. 1); Goff (1990), ch. 3. As a 'historical' account of cultural origins Girard's model is open to serious doubt; my use of it in what follows is based solely on the claim that it is a productive tool for the analysis of imperial epic. If Girard is in the end a mythologist rather than an anthropologist, his is a mythology that seems to have been shared by Romans of the early principate.

the struggle to assert the Trojans' right to this land is sealed with another act of sacrifice. Here, as so often, Virgil is in tune with what was to become a central and abiding mark of the principate, the dominant role of the emperor as sacrificant, symbol of the religious unity of the empire.[6]

Girard develops his theory largely on the basis of the Attic tragic texts, and points to the phenomenon whereby 'In Greek tragedy violence invariably effaces the differences between antagonists' (p. 47). In the *Aeneid* too the concept of the 'sacrificial crisis' can be a powerful tool for analysing the tendency of the two sides to become indistinguishable in their violence and *furor*; that this is so is one of the signs of Virgil's radical contamination of epic with tragedy. The link between the Girardian sacrificial crisis and the very prevalent critical perplexity about making moral distinctions between Aeneas and Turnus is drawn perceptively and in depth in an important article by C. Bandera.[7] 'Virgil is making Aeneas fight his own double, his enemy twin' (233). Bandera's insights may be pressed much further into the detail of the text of the *Aeneid*, and also widened out to provide a key to central features of the post-Virgilian tradition. Or, to turn it round, modern readers will find in the epics of Lucan, Statius, Valerius Flaccus and Silius Italicus some of the most penetrating readings available of the *Aeneid*.

It is a matter of perspective: from some angles Aeneas and Turnus are sharply distinguished, from others they merge into one figure, the more so the more closely they come into contact. This final coming together is narrated in the sequence at 12.672–727. First Turnus rushes to confront Aeneas like a boulder hurtling down a mountain-side, and then Aeneas turns to meet the challenge, like a great mountain. Here the difference is as important as the similarity: both rock-like, but the one rushing down in a one-way journey, the other an immovable peak. The two men now come together in the field of vision of one man, Latinus (707–9): 'Latinus himself is aghast that these two huge heroes, born at opposite ends of the earth, should have come together to decide the issue with iron' *stupet ipse Latinus\ingentis, genitos* diuersis *partibus orbis,\inter se* coiisse uiros et cernere ferro.[8] The rare use of the simple verb *cernere* for the compound

[6] Gordon (1990), 201–31. On the links between the 'sacrifice' of Palinurus and historical sacrifices by Octavian, see Brenk (1988).
[7] Bandera (1981). For an interesting discussion of sacrifice in the *Aeneid* from other points of view, see O'Hara (1990).
[8] Echoed at Silius 16.531 'these well-matched pairs decided the issue with iron' *hi creuere pares ferro*, of the participants in the swordplay at Scipio's games, in which

22

decernere in the sense 'fight out' draws attention to a pun in the word: *cerno* literally means 'sift, separate'; these two have come together (*coiisse*) to make a separation or distinction, but through violence rather than moral or intellectual criteria. The confusion of violence from which will emerge finally the resolution of Turnus' 'sacrifice' is then described (713–14): 'Then with their swords they redouble their shower of blows. Chance and courage are one indistinguishable blur' *tum crebros ensibus ictus|cong*eminant, *fors et uirtus* miscetur in unum.[9] The reader is then invited to look at the two through another simile that eliminates all possibility of distinguishing between them: they are like two bulls fighting for control of the woodland and the herds. This simile points in the direction both of Greek tragedy and of Roman history: the chorus in the first stasimon of Sophocles' *Trachiniae* (508–22) describes the fight between Heracles and Achelous (for a woman) in such a way that Heracles almost merges into the bull form of his adversary. *Aeneid* 12.719, describing the heifers watching fearfully to see 'who will rule in the wood', alludes to Ennius' account of the spectators waiting for the outcome of the auspices of Romulus and Remus – competitors who could not be more closely related.[10]

The image of the two bulls will, recurrently, be that used by Statius for the war between the brothers Polynices and Eteocles, above all in the ravings of the Bacchant queen at *Thebaid* 4.396–402:[11] 'You come upon me; it was a different kind of frenzy that I vowed to you, Bacchus. I see two bulls of a kind clash: both have the same rank, by descent their blood is one; their foreheads meet as they mingle their lofty horns and die fiercely in an alternation of anger. But you are more to blame, give way

the main match is that between two Spanish brothers who use the occasion to settle a dispute (538 *discrimine*) over a disputed throne. The passage is written with more than an eye to Statius' narrative of the duel between Polynices and Eteocles at *Theb.* 11.497–573.

[9] A similar confusion of *uirtus* with something else occurs when the Trojans make themselves visually indistinguishable from the Greeks by putting on Greek armour, 2.390 'trickery or courage – when it's a question of the enemy, who will ask?' *dolus an uirtus, quis in hoste requirat?* This deliberate 'dissolution of differences' is an ironic image of civil war.

[10] 'All men's thought was which one would turn out the ruler' *omnibus cura uiris uter esset induperator*, Enn. *Ann.* 78 Skutsch. Ovid in his narrative of the fight between Hercules and Achelous at *Met.* 9.46–9 imitates both the Ennian passage and *Aen.* 12.715–24.

[11] The Virgilian model is combined with that of the *matrona's* vision of civil war at Lucan 1.674–95.

you who guiltily try to make the ancestral meadows and the family mountainside an exclusion zone to lord over alone'

> en urges; *alium* tibi, Bacche, furorem
> iuraui: *similes* uideo concurrere tauros;
> *idem ambobus* honos *unus*que ab origine sanguis;
> ardua conlatis obnixi cornua *miscent*
> frontibus *alterna*que truces moriuntur in ira.
> tu peior, tu cede, nocens qui *solus* auita
> gramina *communem*que petis defendere montem.

The 'alternation of anger' marks no 'stable difference', only a 'revolving opposition';[12] the Maenad's shot at making *some* distinction in 401–2 repeats Anchises' attempt to separate Caesar and Pompey at *Aeneid* 6.834: 'You hold back first, you' tu*que prior,* tu *parce.*

In Valerius Flaccus the climactic struggle also involves two bulls, 7.539–643, here mastered by a third party, Jason, in the civilizing act of yoking for ploughing. But (abetted by Medea's magic) Jason's determined single-mindedness in taming the fire-breathing bulls issues in the divisions (and misperceptions) of civil war, as the Sown Men who spring from the teeth of the dragon are provoked to turn on one another (638–41): 'Medea forces the wretched brothers to fight themselves. Each of them thought his sword brought down Jason, their anger brought death to them all. Aeetes was aghast, and himself he longed to call the men back from their battle-lust' (*stupet Aeetes ultroque furentes*|*ipse uiros reuocare cupit*: cf. *Aen.* 12.707). Aeetes' amazement is that of Latinus.[13] In the last line of the book the confusion of anger spreads further, as we see Thessalian and Colchian go their separate ways, yet yoked together in their mutual hostility, 653 'both departed with fierce looks, both with threats' ambo *truces,* ambo *abscessere minantes.*

Silius offers two versions of Virgil's final confrontation. Scipio and Hannibal almost come to blows at Cannae, 9.434–7: 'They stood there, the greatest warriors that earth ever saw meet in battle, raised in opposite parts of the world (*educti diuersis orbis in oris*), *equal* in fighting ability, but otherwise the Italian general had the edge, superior in piety and trustworthiness' *melior pietate fideque.* Here the distinction is hardly a problem; the final confrontation of the two men is postponed for Zama,

---

[12] Girard (1977), 149.

[13] This fratricide arises from the same false conviction of other-directed violence as at Cyzicus: see p. 87 below.

at the moment that decides (*discrimen*) who rules the world, 17.385–405. Both generals wear purple – the Punic colour! In the minds of the spectators the two generals are virtually interchangeable, at least in terms of military ability: 402–5 'Had Scipio been born in Africa, they thought that empire would have gone to the descendants of Agenor [Carthaginians]; had Hannibal been born in Italy they did not doubt that the world would have been under Italian jurisdiction'.

Ovid had in fact already inaugurated this line of readings of *Aeneid* 12 at *Metamorphoses* 14.568–72: 'Turnus presses on with the war. Each side has its gods and, something as powerful as gods, the will to fight. And now their goal is not the kingdom that comes with the dowry, nor the father-in-law's throne; it is not your virginity that they desire, Lavinia, but victory, and shame at the thought of stopping the war makes them carry on.'[14] In Lucan the deception involved in making distinctions when the war is a civil war is laid bare in the opposing leaders' speeches to their troops. Caesar appeals to violence as the only source of 'just' decisions (7.259–62): 'This is the day that will prove, with Fate as witness, who took up arms with more justice; this battle (*acies*) will make the defeated into the guilty party. If for my sake you attacked your fatherland with steel and fire, now fight fiercely and absolve yourselves of blame with the sword.'[15] Moral questions are decided simply by the event, *facta*, retrospectively justified as *fatum*. *Acies* means both 'battle-line' and also 'cutting-edge' as of a razor; matters stand on a razor's edge, innocence and guilt to be decided by this day's work. That is one point of view; the alternative concludes Pompey's musings on the no-win situation that he finds himself in (120–3): 'When today's disaster has run its course the name of Pompey will either be universally hated or pitied: to the vanquished will come every ill that a desperate lot (*sors*) brings, to the victor the blame for every crime (*nefas*).' The outcome will be the work of chance (*sors*), not of fate; instead of a judgment in accordance with *fatum* the victory will be a *nefas*.

Lucan's Caesar appeals to an abstract Fate as witness to the justice of his case, as if in a law-court. In a more traditional epic the ultimate source for a critical judgment might be sought transcendentally in the supreme god. It is at this point that Virgil introduces his imitation of the Iliadic weighing by Zeus of the Fates of Achilles and Hector (12.725–7) 'Jupiter

---

[14] Quoted by Quint (1991), 54.

[15] Caesar transgressively asks for the judgment that the epic narrator abjures as forbidden knowledge at 1.126–8 (as Stephen Hinds points out).

himself levelled the balance and lifted up the two pans, placing on them the opposing fates of the two men, to see who was doomed in the struggle and which way death's weight would sink'

> Iuppiter ipse *duas aequato* examine lances
> sustinet et fata imponit *diuersa duorum*,
> quem damnet labor et quo uergat pondere letum.

Virgil goes far beyond Homer in his emphasis on words of duality, and his language hints at the additional notion of the scales of justice; notoriously he also elides the Homeric sequel that tells of a decisive movement of the scales in one direction or the other to 'condemn'. At this critical moment and before the ultimate arbiter of distinctions we are left literally in suspense. 'Total annihilation and salvation are equally balanced on the scales of destiny. At that moment, and only at that moment, can it be said that the smallest possible difference can make, literally, all the difference in the world. All it takes . . . is just one nod, either to the right or to the left, by almighty Jupiter.'[16] We will also remember Jupiter's refusal to take sides at 10.108: 'Be he Trojan or Italian, I will make no distinction' *Tros Rutulusne fuat, nullo discrimine habebo.*

Instead of the final judgment in the court of Olympus Virgil's narrative delivers the finality of violence on earth. The action replays of this human decision by epic imitators and modern critics are seemingly endless, as if the scales of Jupiter hung forever poised, always just on the point of tilting. The problem of discriminating between the actors has its narrative correlative in the way in which the landscape itself is stripped of the marks of religious and legal distinctiveness, firstly at 12.770–1 when the Trojans 'indiscriminately' (*nullo discrimine*) rip out a tree sacred to Faunus 'in order that they might join battle on an open field' (*puro ut possent* con*currere campo*); and secondly at 12.897–8 in Turnus' futile attempt to hurl at Aeneas 'a huge ancient stone, which happened to lie on the battlefield placed there as the boundary-marker of an estate to settle disputes over land' (*limes agro positus litem ut* discerneret[17] *aruis*).

---

[16] Bandera (1981), 234. The indecision of the critics attempting to pass judgment on this passage affords a naughty pleasure: Forbiger takes the absence of a tilt one way or the other as a sign of the epic's incompletion. In 727 there is a much vexed textual problem as to whether to read *et* or *aut:* Warde Fowler concludes 'it is here impossible to be certain'.

[17] The noun *discrimen* is derived from the verb *discerno*.

All for One/One for All

Bandera locates the onset of the 'sacrificial crisis' much earlier in the *Aeneid* than the aborted *foedus* at the beginning of book 12 to which I have referred above, in the failure of the Trojans in book 2 to kill (sacrifice) Sinon, who appears 'bearing all the marks of the sacrificial victim, including the ritual ribbons on his head'.[18] Perhaps one should push the beginning of trouble much further back, to the initial sacrifice of Iphigeneia which set the whole business in motion (*Aen.* 2.116–19); which is to say that the first link in the 'sacrificial' chain of the *Aeneid* coincides with that of Aeschylus' *Oresteia*, a work with which the Latin epic has so much else in common.[19]

Lucretius seems to enter a protest against this kind of beginning when he begins his own 'narrative' (after the proem 1.1–61) with the juxtaposition of two stories of inaugural slaughter, Epicurus' 'killing' of the dragon (or giant) of superstition and Agamemnon's sacrifice of his daughter. Epicurus' journey outwards and upwards leads to the killing that is the necessary prerequisite for the reader's philosophical journey. Lucretius recognizes (80–2) 'that you may think that you are entering on the impious first-principles of reason and setting off on a path of crime'; rather the 'path of crime' is to be identified with the journey of the Greek fleet to Troy (100), made possible by the killing of Iphianassa (Iphigeneia), an episode that brings about the inversion of marriage as funeral, whereas Epicurus' expedition inverts the relative positions of *religio* and mankind. It is the Epicurean journey that is in truth 'prosperous and well-omened'. Lucretius has his eye on the account of the sacrifice of Iphigeneia in Euripides' *Iphigeneia at Aulis*, which tells of Agamemnon's turning away and veiling of his head from the sight of his daughter at the altar (1547–50), a detail which has been used to date this passage of the play as subsequent to the fame of Timanthes' much copied and discussed painting of the scene. While this detail is not made explicit in Lucretius, *maestum* 'mournful' of Agamemnon at 89 may point to it; this may give extra point to the emphasis on Epicurus' willingness to stare out the monster of religion (66–7).[20] More tentatively one might ask

---

[18] Bandera (1981), 235.   [19] See Hardie (1991a).

[20] Laocoon might also be seen as a failed Epicurus, rushing in as 'the first man', *primus*, to confront the Horse, like *Religio* a sky-reaching monster that looms over the city of men (*Aen.*2.47, 186); this lends allusive point to Priam's innocent question to Sinon at 151 'what religious scruple [led the Greeks to construct the Horse]?' *quae*

whether the breakdown of social and religious order in the plague at the end of the *De rerum natura* functions as an image of sacrificial crisis; for Girard the plagues of myth are often symbols of the sacrificial crisis.

Sinon's fiction makes particularly clear the nature of the surrogate victim, or scapegoat, in this case the one man who is a conduit for the fear and violence of the many. When Calchas at Ulysses' prompting finally marks out Sinon as the chosen one, (2.130–1) '*all* consented, and the fate that each man had feared for himself, they did not oppose when turned to the death of *one* poor wretch'. Sinon is a focus for the play of 'one/many' *unus/omnes*: in his own fiction he becomes the scapegoat who alone suffers for the salvation of the generality; he appeals to his Trojan audience to regard him as singular in not being a typical Greek (2.102), 'if you place all Greeks under one heading' *si* omnis uno *ordine habetis Achiuos*; but with the wisdom of hindsight Aeneas recognizes him as a completely typical representative of his race (2.65–6), 'from the crime of one learn what all Greeks are like' *crimine ab* uno/*disce* omnis.[21]

But Sinon frustrates the Greeks' unanimous purpose (134): 'I confess, I snatched myself from the hands of death and burst my chains' *eripui, fateor, leto me et uincula rupi*. This is the escape denied to Turnus by Aeneas (12.947–9): 'are you to be snatched from me (eripiare *mihi*) wearing the spoils of my friends? With this wound Pallas, Pallas sacrifices you.'[22] The successful 'sacrifice' of Turnus brings to an end the series of misfortunes inaugurated by the failure to sacrifice Sinon. At the end the Rutulian general is an unwilling victim, but earlier he has repeatedly offered himself as the one man on behalf of his community in language that reflects, if with Turnus' skewed view of reality, the specifically Roman version of the scapegoat or *pharmakos*, the self-sacrifice of *deuotio*;[23] for example at 11.440–2, 'I Turnus have devoted (*deuoui*) this

---

religio? But Laocoon's reasonable arguments are ignored; where Epicurus had burst out of the walls of the world to destroy Religion, the Horse is introduced amidst religious celebration within the dismantled walls of Troy.

[21] Vida uses the Virgilian Sinon episode to construct his narrative of Christ, the sacrificial lamb, brought before Pilate, *Christiad* 2.966–1001.

[22] *immolo* comes from *mola*, the 'salted barley' *salsae fruges* (2.133), sprinkled on the head of the sacrificial victim, from which Sinon escapes.

[23] Pascal (1990) reviews the earlier discussions and rightly points out the lack of an exact fit between Turnus' behaviour and that of a Decius, but the point may be precisely that Turnus fails through not living up to the selflessness of a *dux deuotus* (balancing the failure of the Trojans to 'sacrifice' Sinon to their advantage at the beginning). For a wide-ranging discussion of the implications of *deuotio* see Versnel

life of mine to you and to my father-in-law Latinus.' At the point where he recognises that his alone is the responsibility for the issue of the war Turnus uses the language of uniqueness (12.694–6): '"It is fairer that I, *one* man, should atone on your behalf for the broken treaty and decide the issue with steel (*decernere ferro*)." They *all* went away from the middle of the battlefield and made space for him.' Here the language of the sacrificial victim and the language of the pre-eminent hero coincide: *unus pro omnibus* may refer either to the epic warrior in his *aristeia* fighting on behalf of his people, or to the scapegoat singled out to bear the guilt of his community. Aeneas' other main opponent, Dido, is also implicated in sacrificial singularity; her suicide is a perversion of, or substitute for, the sacrifice to Stygian Jupiter (4.638–9) that she deceives Anna into thinking that she is going to undertake, and some see in her death a self-sacrifice that will ensure the future potency of her city's revenge on the Romans, whose dead Dido anticipates as sacrificial offerings (*munera* 4.624) to her own shade.[24] As representative of her city Dido sacrifices herself to ensure the future sacrifice of Romans to herself; eventually the death of this one woman will involve the whole of her people in destruction.

Dido's thirst for blood is one of the points of reference for the extensive sacrificial imagery in Lucan's *Bellum Ciuile*. Ahl discusses the notion of the blood spilt in the civil war as offerings to the ghosts of Africa, which he links to the pervasive gladiatorial imagery in the poem through the actual ritual origin of gladiatorial games (*munera*) as funeral offerings to the dead.[25] Ahl fails to note the degree to which Lucan is preceded here by Virgil. As his text for the Lucanian conceit Ahl takes Horace *Odes* 2.1.25–8 'Juno and the gods friendly to Africa who, powerless, had left the unavenged land, gave the conquerors' grandsons as an offering to the shade of Jugurtha.' That the Roman *civil* wars should be a blood-offering to the ghost of Jugurtha (or Hannibal) is an extension of the Virgilian aetiology of the Hannibalic war as satisfaction for the ghost of Dido (sacrifice calling forth further sacrifice in the manner of an Aeschylean trilogy). In her Cassandran curse Dido looks for an avenger to rise from

(1981). Another victim of devotion may be Marcellus: Servius on 1.712 'devoted to the coming plague' *pesti deuota futurae* says that the phrase was taken from Augustus' funeral speech for Marcellus, 'when he said that he was devoted to a premature death' *immaturae morti deuotum fuisse*. Virgil presents Marcellus as a kind of offering to divert the envy of the gods at 6.870–1.

[24] Tupet (1970), 253–6; Grottanelli (1972).   [25] Ahl (1976), ch. 3.

her bones, and calls on her people actively and eternally to prosecute her hatred of the race of Aeneas. Ahl also overlooks the importance of the gladiatorial arena as one of the images under which war in the *Aeneid* is viewed.[26]

Of all the first-century epicists Lucan explores most insistently the topic of the sacrifice of the one for the many. Sacrificial violence rioting beyond any possible limits and the attempt by one man to limit its fury to himself form the subject of the first half of the second book in two contrasting episodes. In the first (2.67–233) an old man remembers the civil war between Marius and Sulla, examples for the present fear (2.67). Marius is a victim who has escaped, like Virgil's Sinon;[27] in the balance-sheet of fate many other deaths are owing before the death of this one man can be countenanced (82–3): countless dead while one man survives. The ensuing slaughter makes no discrimination between rank or age; human blood is shed in the temples (103) instead of the acceptable blood of animal victims. Scaevola is killed before the altar of Vesta in a replay of the Virgilian death of Priam at his altar. Marius' opponent Sulla is no different: the *pièce de résistance* of his proscriptions is the death of Marius Gratidianus, offered as a sacrificial victim to placate the shade of Catulus (173–6), one man killed by a thousand cuts (186–7) unum|tot *poenas cepisse caput*).[28] There follows the slaughter of all the inhabitants of Praeneste at one single point of time (195 unius *populum pereuntem tempore mortis*).

From the universal panic caused by the recollection of these examples two just men are exempt, Brutus and Cato. In this episode (2.234–325) the dialectic of *unus/omnes* is as sharply focused on Cato as it is on Caesar, of whom Cato is (or should be) the negative image.[29] Brutus

---

[26] Though he does note, 86 n. 8 'The early *munera* were fought in the Forum Boarium, the legendary site of the fight between Hercules and Cacus. Hence the Hercules–Cacus fight may well have been very closely associated with the idea of a gladiatorial *munus*.'

[27] Servius sees in *Aen.* 2.135 'hiding for the night in the sedge of a muddy swamp' *limosoque lacu per noctem obscurus in ulua* (Sinon escaping from being sacrificed) an allusion to the story of Marius; Lucan echoes the Virgilian line at 2.70 'the exiled Marius hid his head in the muddy sedge' *exul limosa Marius caput abdidit ulua*. Servius also notes the Virgilian allusion to the death of Pompey in the description of the headless trunk of Priam, an allusion similarly 'rehistoricized' by Lucan in his narrative of the original historical model.

[28] On this and other civil war human sacrifices, see Weinstock (1971), 398 f.

[29] See p. 11 above.

appeals to Cato to remain aloof from the civil war in an Olympian isolation; Cato replies with a 'holy utterance' (285) but rejects the invitation to a divine distance from events. He sees himself rather in the role of a 'father of the fatherland' (*pater patriae*) who cannot stay away from his children's funeral (297–302); if the gods demand 'Roman expiatory victims' (304), then Cato will not cheat the account of his blood. So far Cato has parried Brutus' praise of his singularity with the desire to be just one more Roman who collectively must pay for past crimes;[30] now he changes tack and accepts, or wishes for, the role of *unus*, but as the one victim whose death will pay for all of Rome. Where Marius Gratidianus had been the one man whom a thousand 'deaths' doomed as a probably unacceptable offering to the ghost of the one man Catulus, and then only as a particular instance of the universal slaughter of Romans, Cato longs, Decius-like (307–11), to be the single target of Roman and barbarian weapons in order to be the universal scapegoat and saviour. As sacrificial mediator he will provide the necessary discrimination between the twinned armies of civil war (309–11): 'Let the twin armies transfix me . . . Place me in the middle that I may receive the wounds of the whole war' (another version of death by a thousand cuts).[31] In 314–19 the rhetoric of the scapegoat is given an ironic twist; given that the peoples of the earth are ready to become the willing slaves of a monarch, the further shedding of blood is pointless, except in the case of Cato who alone and futilely stands for laws and liberty. His sacrificial throat (317 *iugulus*) will in these circumstances yield peace and 'an end to the evils' (*finemque malorum* 317), as the death of Turnus is the *finis* of the *Aeneid*. In the event the manner of Cato's death was such as to rule out absolutely any possibility of a resolution to the sacrificial crisis; turning his hand on himself, acting out the roles of both sacrificer and sacrificed in one person, he confounded utterly the distinction between killer and killed on which the logic of Girardian victimization rests. The last words of Cato's speech in book 2 reveal again the close connection between the singularity of the scapegoat and of the 'royal metaphor' (322–3): 'Then let him conquer with me as one of his soldiers, lest he imagine that it was for himself that he conquered.' By standing out alone

---

[30] Cf. Verg. *Geo.* 1.501–2 (praying that Octavian come as the unique saviour from civil war) 'for long enough we have been paying for the perjury of Laomedon's Troy with *our* blood'.

[31] Just as to start with (1.100) Crassus, the third *triumuir*, had been 'in the middle, a stay against war'.

as the one 'soldier' who is not just the passive instrument of his general, Cato will ensure that in victory Pompey cannot represent himself to himself as the solipsistic *unus homo*.[32]

Sacrifice and substitution 1

In the *Aeneid* 'the general sacrificial law' (Bandera 223) is most clearly formulated in Neptune's words to Venus at 5.814–15 promising a safe journey for the Trojans from Sicily to Italy: 'there will be just one whom you will miss, lost at sea; one life will be given for many' unus *erit tantum amissum quem gurgite quaeres;*|unum *pro* multis *dabitur caput*. This is the inverse of Juno's envious version of the death of Oilean Ajax, where the whole fleet is involved in the punishment of the one sinner. The victim in book 5 will turn out to be not quite arbitrary: Palinurus is the helmsman, the one man who should be responsible for the safety of the whole ship; the symbolic value of his office is made clear when the place of the lost Palinurus is taken by the *unus homo* himself, Aeneas, guiding the 'ship of state' safely to Italy.[33]

Sacrifice operates through substitution and exchange;[34] the victim is offered in exchange for benefits or in payment of a negative balance incurred through earlier crimes. The victim itself has a symbolic value, standing in as a surrogate for those who offer it. The Palinurus episode reveals a chain of such substitutions and exchanges. He is the price exacted in return for the safe arrival in Italy of the rest of the Trojans. But substitution also extends to disguise and role-playing: the god of sleep, *Somnus*, disguised as, or playing the part of, the human Phorbas, offers himself deceptively as a substitute helmsman while Palinurus takes on the part of sleep (846 'I myself will carry out your duties on your behalf for a while'). Sleep, as we know, is the close brother of Death, and here is

---

[32] The difference between Pompey and Cato is pointed by the contrast between 2.321 'he even promises himself jurisdiction of the whole world' (Pompey) and 383 (Cato) 'he believed that he had been born to serve not himself but the whole world'. For other examples of the play on *dux/miles*, see p. 7 above.

[33] See Lossau (1980), 110 on the parallel between Palinurus and Elpenor as 'companions' of their respective leaders, Elpenor like Patroclus going to the Underworld before his master. In the *Odyssey* the one man Odysseus reaches home safely, while the Phaeacian ship that carried him is the victim of Poseidon's anger.

[34] Hubert & Mauss (1964), 10 point to this aspect of sacrifice, which they describe as 'this succession of representations which we shall encounter at every one of the stages of sacrifice'.

another disguise, for what Somnus really offers is not forty winks but the forgetfulness of death. Palinurus himself functions as a kind of twin of Aeneas; his death is a substitute for the latter's death and precondition for his fated success (as the success of Romulus arose out of the death of his twin).[35] When Palinurus has fallen overboard his place and office are taken by Aeneas (868): 'he himself (*ipse*) steered the ship over the waves through the night,' as if through this chain of substitutions we finally arrive at a halting-place, the man 'himself' (*ipse uir*).

The shifting identifications in the death of Palinurus provide a model for a reading of the final 'sacrifice' of the poem, a play of substitution in which neither the victim Turnus *nor* the slayer is wholly himself. Turnus loses his life because he is wearing another man's armour, the swordbelt of Pallas; and by doing so he transfers to himself the symbolism of the ephebe cut down on his wedding night contained in the swordbelt's scene of the Danaids. In reminding Aeneas of what is most dear to him this has the effect of alienating Aeneas from himself, both in the sense, often noted, that he loses control of his emotions, and through his appropriation of another's name for his decisive action. 'Pallas, Pallas [not 'Aeneas'] sacrifices you.' The effect of proper name as subject of a third-person verb juxtaposed with the second person (*Pallas te*) is heightened by Aeneas' extremely personal use of first- and second-person pronouns in the preceding question (12.947–9): 'Are you, wearing the spoils of my friends, to be snatched from me? Pallas sacrifices you, Pallas, with this wound.' t*une hinc spoliis indute* meorum|*eripiare* mihi? *Pallas te hoc uulnere,* Pallas|*immolat*. These substitutions have their Iliadic background: Pallas plays the role of (is a Virgilian substitution for) Patroclus, the *therapon* of Achilles who goes into battle wearing the armour of Achilles. Patroclus is an *alter ego* of Achilles who dies in his stead (and whose death is also a prefiguration of Achilles' own death), and it is probable that in Homer the literary motif of the *alter ego* conceals an older practice of the ritual substitution of a human victim for the king who should die.[36] Furthermore the use here of the name Pallas is itself a Virgilian appropriation of an Iliadic passage that talks of surrogate action and compensation: at *Iliad* 22.270–2 Achilles tells Hector 'There is no longer any escape for you; Pallas Athene will

---

[35] *Aen.* 5.814 is yet another echo of Ennius *Ann.* 54 Skutsch (see p. 6 above): this and other aspects of Palinurus as double of Aeneas are well discussed by Nicoll (1988).

[36] Whitman (1958), 136 ff., 200 ff; on *therapon*, see Lowenstam (1981), drawing on van Brock (1959); Nagy (1979), 292–3.

straightway conquer you with my spear, and now you will pay back all the deaths of my companions whom you killed with the spear in your battle rage.'[37] Through the homonymy of the name Pallas, Virgil substitutes a mortal youth for the warrior goddess; but this is a substitution that also operates within the text of the *Aeneid* itself, for, if the poem ends with the hero killing his enemy in the name of Pallas, it had begun with Aeneas' enemy Juno's wish that she could kill him in a repetition of the punishment of Oilean Ajax – by none other than *Pallas* (Athena), 1.39.

Virgil sharpens the Homeric model and gives it greater emphasis by choosing to end his epic in a hall of mirrors where identity is split. This last scene of the *Aeneid* pulls in (at least) two directions at once. On one level the final encounter of Aeneas and Turnus is the most personal episode in the poem. The dispute has been resolved on the divine level, and the one remaining divine actress, Juturna, has been pulled out; we are left with the individual Aeneas facing the individual Turnus. But both humans are acting out other roles than their own, wearing other disguises and masks, Aeneas above all as an *Ersatz*-Achilles to Turnus' Hector; as vicariously performing the will of Jupiter; and, by his own words, as the re-embodiment of the dead Pallas. Instead of Aeneas facing Turnus we might see this as two versions of Pallas opposing each other, Aeneas as the agent of Pallas' revenge and Turnus as the young warrior who, by foolishly dressing in the sword-belt of Pallas, has consigned himself to the same premature and pathetic death in battle as his victim. Once more the collapse of distinctions that results from the play of literary models seems to coincide with a feature of sacrificial practice as analysed by Hubert and Mauss in their chapter on 'Sacrifice of the God': (p. 85) 'the priest can be an incarnation of the god as well as the victim: often he disguises himself in the god's likeness'; (p. 88) 'Priest or victim, priest and victim, it is a god already formed that both acts and suffers in the sacrifice.'

In the final fulfilment of his mission in Italy, and when he should be most true to himself, Aeneas as sacrificer is caught up in a logic of sacrificial substitution. This is disturbing if a central subject of the *Aeneid* (as of the *Odyssey*) is 'the man (himself)' (*uirum, Aen.* 1.1); the epic will set about defining that man, its hero, but ends only by placing his identity in doubt. 'Who is Augustus and what does he stand for, and what indeed is his name?' were the questions that pressed on Virgil's contemporary audience, and the definition of the emperor was to remain problematical.

[37] The unexpected plural *meorum* at *Aen.* 12.947 is a memory of Achilles' ἐμῶν ἑτάρων.

On the literary–historical level, epic closure is thwarted, allowing for the possibility of an indefinite series of replays in epics after the *Aeneid* as the Roman epic hero constantly seeks to define his own identity through the impersonation of earlier historical and literary models; perhaps as each successive Roman emperor sought the appropriate self-representation, defining his own closeness to, or distance from, the first emperor Augustus.

Possession and impersonation

Sacrificial substitution is a special case of the recurrent appearance in the Latin epic of the phenomena of possession and impersonation. These features represent at the level of the individual actor the characteristics of repetition and imitation, foregrounded in epic for reasons discussed in chapter I. When a human actor repeats or imitates a personal model by entering into the latter's substance (impersonation) or by being invaded by the prior person (possession), then we may say that the drives towards totalization and continuation coincide, through an act of appropriation. Yet the resulting personal totality is always in a relation of dependence, and hence incompleteness, in regard to the prior person. For example, Lucan's hyperbolic parody of the epic *unus homo*, Scaeva, achieves his unique status as the result of a chain of substitutions: Scaeva stands in for Caesar, who in turn stands in for the multitudes of soldiers under his command. But Scaeva has no justification for his existence *except* as an *alter Caesar*.

Epic impersonation may be traced to a number of grounds other than the logic of sacrifice discussed above. In literary terms it is the result of the devoted epicist's imitation of the heroes created by his predecessors. Aeneas' status as the *unus homo* is partly intelligible as the result of his appropriation of the virtues (and failings) of the most notable of earlier epic heroes – Ulysses, Achilles, Ajax, Hector, Menelaus, Agamemnon, etc. The process has gone so far that it is difficult to locate a central and stable ground of Aeneas' identity, which may partly explain the problems that readers so often have in identifying with Aeneas. Another source is the ideal, particularly dear to the Romans, of the preservation of family identity through the (male) succession of generations.[38] In the *Aeneid* this is thematized in the person of Neoptolemus whose success in living up to his father Achilles is the subject of a bitter exchange of taunts with his

---

[38] On this, very trenchant comments in Griffin (1985), 183–97.

victim Priam (2.533–50).[39] The voice of the narrator adds its own gloss in the simile at 2.471–5 comparing Neoptolemus to a snake that emerges from its winter hiding-place with renewed youth after shedding its skin, an image that points to the notion of literal rebirth. Another supernatural model for reincarnation is the survival of the dead in the form of a Fury; this is of such importance for the Latin epic that I shall reserve it for a separate section.

This may be another area where the influence of the stage is visible: Virgil at several points plays with the literal sense of 'impersonation' as 'the wearing of masks', above all in the figure of Dido, whose story, as is well-known, is narrated with many tragic resonances. In the unusual simile at 4.469–73 Dido in her distress is compared to famous characters from the tragic stage, alerting the reader to the way in which the stage-convention of masking enters the 'real world' of the epic narrative as Dido tries on a number of roles, with disastrous results.[40] Another 'mask' that many characters in Latin epic try on for size is that of Hercules; often the interest centres on the success or failure of such attempts to play a part. In Valerius Flaccus' *Argonautica* the disappearance of Hercules is followed by a debate as to whether the heroes that remain can fill the Herculean role (see especially 3.667–75, 712–14); a partial answer is provided in the next book when Pollux wins a very Herculean victory in the boxing-match against the monstrous Bebrycian king Amycus.[41] There is even the possibility of characters attempting to live up to their own roles – in earlier literary treatments of their own stories – in a displacement on to his characters of the poet's attempt to rival *his* predecessor. The most striking expression of this kind of role-playing comes from a tragedy rather than epic, the exultant cry of Seneca's Medea, 'Now I am Medea' *Medea nunc sum* (*Medea* 910), as she finally realizes her 'character', but the phenomenon is also found in epic, particularly in Statius.[42] In all of this one may discern an analogy with the political 'reality' of the early principate, whose success depended to a large extent on the correct choice from, and enactment of, a variety of roles for the ruler. Nero's stagey life and death are but the logical conclusion of a tendency inherent in the principate from the beginning.[43]

---

[39] See pp. 89–90 below.   [40] Hardie (1991b).

[41] For the epic hero as imitator of Hercules, see pp. 66–7 below.

[42] Feeney (1991), 343 on the way in which Statius' characters 'intermittently share their creator's heightened awareness of the history which they inhabit'. Henderson (1991), 67 n. 61, speaks of this intertextuality as the 'topology of present absence'.

[43] Note also the strange doublings of the imperial person catalogued by Kantorowicz (1957), 500 ff., as precedents for the medieval doctrine of the king's two bodies: e.g.

Other impulses to impersonation derive from typical features of epic narrative. The habit of epic gods of disguising themselves as mortals is hinted at in Aeneas' final assumption of a name (Pallas) which is not just that of a young Greek, but also of one of the most powerful Olympians. In Virgil impersonation (the Homeric model) has been converted into possession; Statius takes the cue in one of his imitations of the final Virgilian duel at *Thebaid* 8.457–9: 'Theban Haemon cuts down the Argives and drives them before him; raging Tydeus pursues the Theban lines. The latter enjoys the presence of Pallas, the former is full of Hercules' (*Pallas huic praesens, illum Tirynthius implet*). The confusion of identity that results is highlighted in the sequel when the god 'leaves' Haemon (519–20): 'he sensed that the god was gone; there was less force in his spear-throws and in no stroke did he recognise his own strength of hand' (*nulloque manum cognoscit in ictu*), where the departure of the god seems also to involve departure of his *own* strength. Virgilian allusion continues here, for Haemon suffers Turnus' realization that he is no longer quite himself as he tries to lift a huge stone at *Aeneid* 12.903–4: 'but he did not recognize himself in the way that he ran or walked, or lifted and threw the huge stone from his hand' *sed neque currentem* se nec cognoscit *euntem|tollentemue* manu *saxumue immane mouentem*. The final scene in this drama comes at the end of *Thebaid* 8 with Tydeus' 'recognition of himself' in the severed head of Melanippus (8.753 *seseque adgnouit in illo*).[44] The consequence of this, the cannibalistic gnawing at the head, leads to the abrupt departure of Pallas from her mortal favourite – another comment on the ending of the *Aeneid*.

The epic plot also deals in other types of substitution: the phantom, *eidolon, umbra, imago*, sent by a god to mislead a hero; or the stepping of a lesser warrior into the shoes of a greater, on the model of Patroclus and Achilles. In the *Aeneid* both Pallas and Camilla play the Patroclan role of surrogate victim for their respective chiefs; both characters are entangled in chains of substitution.

The substitutability of the hero at the (or a) climax of the epic is explored also by Lucan, Statius and Silius. In both the *Bellum Ciuile* and the *Punica* the plot denies a fatal encounter between the two chief actors, but

Caligula's dedication of a temple to himself, in which stood a golden image of himself dressed daily with the same clothes as worn that day by the emperor himself (Suet. *Calig.* 22.3). On the emperor's funeral with its double cremation of the imperial body, once in the flesh and once in a wax *imago*, see Dupont (1989) (taking up Kantorowicz). 44 See p. 69 below.

a meeting is engineered by other means. In the *Bellum Ciuile* Pompey dies a Stoic death which is utterly (and allusively) opposed to the impassioned and indignant response of Turnus to his death.[45] His killer is of course not Caesar – at least not literally. Firstly note that Pompey like Turnus, has found his Achilles in the Egyptian Achillas. In the *Bellum Ciuile* the Achillean role is played by Caesar; Achillas is thus a more appropriate murderer than he can know, although he is an adept at role-playing as we see at 10.418–19 'the foreign henchman set about civil war, and Achillas took the role of a Roman' *et in partem Romani uenit Achillas*. But Caesar is doubly present: as he is struck Pompey admonishes himself (8.627–32): 'Do not give in to shame and bemoan the author of your death. However the blows fall, believe that there is the hand of your father-in-law. Let them scatter and mutilate my body, yet, O gods, I am fortunate, and no god has the power to take that from me. In life prosperity admits of alteration, but death brings no misfortune.' In Achillas Pompey can persuade himself to recognize the hand of Caesar. But if the identity of the agent is open to question that of the victim is not: he is – not Pompeius or Magnus indeed, both names (or epithets) open to change in quality or quantity – but 'Fortunate'.[46] On the point of death he appears to escape the epic hero's liability to become other than himself, fixed in his own definition of *felicitas*. And in death even his mutilated physical remains preserve a visible sign of this immutability (665–7): 'Those who gazed on his mutilated head are witness that death's final stroke did not change the hero's composure and look.' But, despite the elaborate *laudatio funebris* that rounds off book 8 of the *Bellum Ciuile*, that is not the end of the story. Pompey will return as we shall see.

In Silius' account of the battle of Zama the final duel between the two generals Hannibal and Scipio is thwarted through a Virgilian substitution: Juno creates a phantom of Scipio to lead Hannibal out of the battle (17.522–33). The re-enactment in Silius' last book of the final duel

[45] Lucan uses the vocabulary of the last line of the *Aeneid*, 'with a groan his life fled indignant down to the shades' *uitaque cum gemitu fugit indignata sub umbras: Bell. Ciu.* 8.619 *nullo* gemitu; 614 indignatus, but Pompey's sense of what he is worth leads him deliberately to shade his face by veiling it in a kind of pre-empting of his death: 615 'he closed his eyes' *lumina pressit* as of the relative closing the eyes of the dead person.

[46] Even in this Pompey is prey to irony, for *felix* is a highly ambivalent (changeable) word in Lucan: see Henderson (1988), 128–9. The shape of line 630 may remind us of that other great epic self-assertion (*Aen.* 1.378) 'I am pious Aeneas' *sum pius Aeneas. Felix* had been the *cognomen* of Sulla.

between Aeneas and Turnus is short-circuited by the substitution of the abortive encounter between Trojan and Rutulian in *Aeneid* 10 for the end-game of *Aeneid* 12. The real Hannibal, after asserting that his fame will be coextensive with the rule of Jupiter, flees out of the epic into 'a safe hiding-place' (617 *tutasque latebras*, the equivalent of the *umbrae* into which the 'life of Turnus' flees in the last line of the *Aeneid*). But this is not the last appearance of Hannibal in the poem: back in Rome the magnet for all minds and eyes at the triumph of Scipio is (644) 'the picture of Hannibal fleeing on the battle-field' *Hannibalis campis fugientis imago* (fleeing after a phantom, one might add), a surrogate for the absent Carthaginian leader. By contrast the next word *ipse* signals the real (if heavily made-up) presence of Scipio, 'he himself standing on his chariot, adorned with gold and purple' ipse, *adstans curru atque auro decoratus et ostro*.[47] The last nine lines of the poem, however, show us not Scipio himself, but a series of *imagines*, similes and comparisons, substitutes for the historical man. The face that the Romans look on is that of Mars (646); Scipio in triumph is like Bacchus or Hercules; he is no whit inferior to Romulus or to Camillus. These comparisons are the justification for the final claim (653–4): 'Nor in truth does Rome invent a son for the Thunderer when she records that you are of divine parentage' *nec uero, cum te memorat de stirpe deorum,|prolem Tarpei mentitur Roma Tonantis*. Scipio's equality (for which one might read the Roman emperor's equality) with gods and heroes legitimizes the final claim of the thundering epic voice that he is the son of Jupiter himself (a claim that presumably no reader will take at face value), and which also reminds us of the historical impersonation of Jupiter by the *triumphator* wearing the *ornatus Iouis*.[48] For all the protestation of *nec uero . . . mentitur*, Scipio is anything but himself, *ipse*. At least the *imago* of Hannibal may be supposed to aim for verisimilitude, creating the same deception of presence that the *effigies* or *simulacrum* of Scipio imposed on the real Hannibal at Zama.

Silius gives us another version of the end of the *Aeneid* in a minor episode in the course of the battle before Nola, 12.212–58, where a

---

[47] The Virgilian model is *Aen.* 8.720 '[Augustus] himself sitting on the snow-white threshold of gleaming Apollo' *ipse sedens niueo candentis limine Phoebi*, where *ipse* and *Phoebi* frame the line and suggest the way in which Augustus is Apollo's vicar on earth. Virgil's *triumphator* is also elusive; at Actium he is given his honorary title *Augustus* (8.678), four years before he actually adopted that stage name. And anyway, all that we see is a set of *imagines* on an imaginary work of art.

[48] Versnel (1970), ch. 2.

Paduan named Pedianus kills a young Carthaginian named Cinyps, a favourite of Hannibal to whom he had given the helmet of Paullus. When Pedianus spies Cinyps wearing the helmet, it is as if the *imago* of Paullus had risen from the world below to demand back his armour. The precise location of the dead man's ghost is uncertain; in Cinyps seem to be combined both the transgressor and the avenging spirit; in 239 the words 'behold Paullus' indicate that Pedianus takes on the role himself, as Aeneas embodies (the almost homonymous!) Pallas at the end of the *Aeneid*, but the next words suggest that the ghost is still elsewhere, 'he calls the hero's shade to watch'. However we read this, the killing of Cinyps separates the beautiful boy from the great consul's armour that he so inappropriately wears. Pedianus, on the other hand, by this exploit justifies *his* claim to wear the armour of another. He is introduced as (212) 'the young man Pedianus in the armour of Polydamas', a Trojan hero, and he himself claims descent from the Trojan Antenor. Marcellus congratulates him for the recovery of Paullus' helmet with an adaptation of Apollo's confirmation of Ascanius' dynastic worth (257–8) 'bravo for the courage of your ancestors, bravo son of Antenor' *macte o uirtutis auitae,|macte Antenoride.*[49] This Paduan wears no borrowed plumes. His success as champion of the dead may have a particular point, for Pedianus is introduced as an honorary ancestor of the Paduan Asconius Pedianus, commentator on Cicero, 'a man who helped preserve Cicero's reputation, just as Silius sought to do for Cicero and Vergil'.[50]

Furies and re-embodiment: the living dead

One way of understanding what happens at the end of the *Aeneid* is to see in the infuriated Aeneas the incarnation of the avenging Erinys or Fury of Pallas.[51] In imperial Latin epic the Furies are the most potent of the various forces of possession and re-embodiment. If we go back to Aeschylus' *Oresteia* we find that the Erinyes are the living force of revenge whose vitality feeds on the repeated deaths of the human actors; whose vitality indeed may be defined almost as the urge to repeat murder. Already in tragedy demonic characters may figuratively be called 'Furies'.[52] In imperial Latin epic the abstract power of the curse[53] has

---

[49] Cf. *Aen.* 9.641 *macte noua uirtute.*

[50] Pomeroy (1990), 133.   [51] Renger (1985), 96–8.

[52] Aesch. *Ag.* 749, 1500–4; Ennius *Alexander* 49 Jocelyn, probably adapted from Euripides' *Alexandros.*

[53] Burkert (1985), 197–8, for the Erinys as 'simply an embodiment of the act of self-cursing contained in the oath'.

become an undying principle of embodiment or re-embodiment. The Fury is like a virus that replicates herself in her victim, often in multiple copies (just as, one might add, Virgil's Allecto episode will reproduce itself in multiple copies in the works of the successors of Virgil). Thus Allecto, called up by Juno in *Aeneid* 7, finally leaves the upper world when she has created versions of herself in Amata, Turnus and the Italian shepherds. A Fury may also be a form of personal survival after death. Dido's curse works through this mechanism. At 4.384–7 she tells Aeneas 'when I am gone I will chase you with black flames, and when cold death has separated my limbs from my soul, I shall be everywhere, a shadow. You will pay the penalty, wicked man; I shall hear of it, and the report will reach me among the shades below'

> . . . sequar atris ignibus absens
> et, cum frigida mors anima seduxerit artus,
> omnibus umbra locis adero. dabis, improbe, poenas.
> audiam et haec Manis ueniet mihi fama sub imos.

The paradoxical nature of this kind of survival is seen in the phrases *sequar absens* and *umbra adero* ('I shall follow in my absence', 'as a shadow I shall be present') which play the 'absent yet present' trick in an inversion of each other.[54] The (equally paradoxical) 'black fires' are the torches of the Fury transferred to the human victim, as they are also in the explicitly mythological tableau at 4.472–3: 'Orestes flees his mother armed with her torches and black snakes, and the avenging Furies sit at the threshold.' Here the simile describes Dido's mental state, but it is also an image of the frenzy which she in turn will wish to inflict on Aeneas. In her final curse Dido foresees herself as a *revenant* (625–6): 'arise, someone, as avenger from my bones, to pursue the Trojan settlers with flame and sword' *exoriare aliquis nostris ex ossibus ultor|qui face Dardanios ferroque sequare colonos*. The living Hannibal-to-be is projected into the future as a Fury-like double of Dido. Newman has suggested that we do indeed find versions of the furious Dido as we read on: Allecto and her victims, above all Turnus who is in many ways the male

---

[54] Henry cites for the notion of 'absent presence' Cic. *pro Milone* 97 'glory is the one thing that offers the memory of posterity as consolation for the shortness of life, that brings it about that, though absent, we are present, though dead, we live' *quae efficeret ut absentes adessemus, mortui uiueremus*. The coincidence of phrasing points to a much wider and persistent association in Latin epic of the powers of the Fury and of *Fama*, as a mythological personification merely the negative aspect of the *fama* that is the *raison d'être* of epic. See ch. 3 for other links between the epic poet and the forces of Hell.

equivalent of Dido in the second half of the poem.[55] At the end the power of Allecto fades from Turnus, as his enemy Aeneas is fired with the frenzy of the 'counter-Fury' sent down by Jupiter. The last embodiment of a Fury in the *Aeneid* is Aeneas himself.

Lucan is a connoisseur of demonic possession. A small example with a great climax, the bad dreams of the Caesarians on the battlefield the night after Pharsalia (7.772–6): 'Sleep brings the hiss of snakes and torch-fires. There is (*adest*) the shade of the slaughtered citizen; each man is pinned down by an incubus of terror. This man looks on the faces of old men, that man sees the shapes of the young, this man is chased through his sleep by the corpses of brothers, that man's breast is filled with his father. Caesar is possessed by the shades of all the dead' (*omnes in Caesare manes*). Here too Caesar's imperialist expansiveness crowds out everyone else. The passage is immediately followed by Lucan's reworking of the 'Orestes and Pentheus possessed' simile, applied by Virgil to Dido.

But the living Caesar had been demonic from the very beginning; it is more surprising to discover that the dead Pompey is also allowed no rest. Despite his proud claim to die *felix*, his posthumous fate is all too like that of Virgil's *infelix Dido*. Book 8 of the *Bellum Ciuile*, as we saw, defined the immutable identity in death of Pompey. At the beginning of the next book his disembodied soul soars free of his sordid earthly remains up to the eternally unchanging stars, the place that is the reward for 'semi-divine shades'. But his stay is brief, for he returns to make a pass over the battlefield before taking up residence in the breast of Brutus and the mind of Cato.[56] These are lofty residences indeed, but Pompey has himself succumbed to the epic law of impersonation and re-embodiment, and, more worryingly still, this monolith of Stoic virtue has split in two. The number of pretenders to the Pompeian spirit multiplies further. Cornelia chides herself for her concern for the externalities of a tomb (9.70–1): 'Is your breast not loaded full with Pompey, forgetful woman?' *non toto in pectore portas,|inpia, Pompeium?* Magnus' instructions as recollected by his sons suggest another form of survival, the demonic possession by the dead of their biological descendants (9.88–90): 'My sons, succeed me in the civil war, and let the Caesars never be free to reign so long as one of my race remains on earth' (*dum terris aliquis nostra de*

[55] Newman (1986), 158.

[56] The effect of this possession is described at 9.23–4 'but after the Thessalian disaster he was whole-heartedly Pompey's' (*pectore toto|Pompeianus erat*: for a similar trick with *Pompeianus* at 6.717, see p. 109 below).

stirpe manebit, recalling Dido's immortalization of herself in her curse at *Aen.* 4.625 *exoriare aliquis nostris ex ossibus ultor*). At 9.17 the phrase 'avenger of crimes' *scelerum uindex* might suggest a Fury rather than a celestial spirit. In book 10 the dead Pompey becomes more Fury-like still: paradoxically averting the expiatory death of Caesar at 6–7: 'Magnus, your shadow saved Caesar, your ghost rescued your father-in-law from slaughter'; possessing the villainous Pothinus at 333–7: 'But Pothinus' crazed thoughts, once infected with sacrilegious murder, did not rest from crime. After the killing of Magnus nothing was taboo for him. The ghost dwells in his breast and the avenging goddesses inspire him with a mad lust for fresh monstrosities' (*habitant sub pectore manes|ultricesque deae dant in noua monstra furorem*). One of the last events before the book breaks off is the killing of Pompey's killer Achillas: 524 'Magnus, another victim is now sacrificed to your shade' *altera, Magne, tuis, iam* uictima *mittitur umbris*. Pompey's shade has now grown as thirsty for blood as the shade of the original Achilles – or, one might add, as the infuriated Aeneas at the end of the *Aeneid*.

In the Lemnian episode in book 2 of Valerius' *Argonautica* Venus inflicts a terrible punishment on the women who have neglected her cult, through a revenger's tragedy of deception and infuriation which alludes constantly to the actions of the mythological Furies, above all through extended imitation of the Allecto episode in *Aeneid* 7 – but in which the one agent *not* literally present is the Fury herself. In the sign-post at the beginning of the story Venus' revenge is labelled 'a Fury-like destruction' *exitium furiale* (2.102); Valerius then informs us that there are two faces of Venus, the face of nurturing beauty such as we see in Lucretius' opening hymn to Venus, and the face that is hardly to be distinguished from the 'virgins of the Styx', that is, the Furies (102–6). Ancient gods traditionally have beneficent and maleficent aspects, but Valerius here goes further in the construction of a split Olympian identity. In literary–historical terms the picture is the product of 'combinatorial imitation' of the *Aeneid*, in which the actions of Venus and Allecto, separately narrated, reveal a disturbing similarity to one another.[57] But Valerius goes beyond Virgil to suggest that Venus has a self-contained *persona* as a 'Fury'. The absent yet possessing Fury multiplies further: Venus' first assault on the women of Lemnos is made through the personification of *Fama* (115–34), portrayed as a combination of three

[57] Hardie (1990b), 5–9; for a discussion of the Allecto-like quality of Venus, see Lyne (1987), 13 ff.

destructive supernatural agents in the *Aeneid*: the Virgilian *Fama*, the winds of Aeolus (rumour is after all 'windy'), and Allecto. *Fama* is mistress of fictions and false characters, and naturally her intervention on earth is in disguise, as one of the Lemnian wives (141), a tactic imitated by Venus (174). The combined effect of these two goddesses is to transform the Lemnian women themselves into versions of Furies (191–5, 237–8; the whole episode is also shot through with echoes of Virgil's Dido and her 'transformation' into a Fury). Identity is constantly threatened. What are we to make of Venus' statement to *Fama* at 134 'shortly I myself shall be there' *mox* ipsa|*adero*, a promise realized in the narrative at 196 with Venus' casting aside of *her* disguise – but only to appear in the 'costume' of the Virgilian Allecto, 'Venus herself (*ipsa Venus*) shaking the waves of fire that jet from her torch'. At this point the poet unexpectedly interjects his own voice (216–19): 'How shall I relate so many faces of crime, so many kinds of death? Ah, to what horrors the story has brought the bard! What a sequence unfolds itself! O, for someone to halt me in my true song and free my nights from these pictures' *o qui me uera canentem|sistat et hac nostras exsoluat imagine noctes!* The poet, claiming disingenuously to be the mouthpiece of a true epic *fama* (as opposed to the indiscriminate utterances of mythological *Fama*, 'singing things both fit and unfit', 117), confuses the night of the Lemnian slaughter with the nights of his poetic labour filled with the theatre of his imagination (*imagine*).[58]

But it is Statius who provides us with the ultimate exploration of the themes of the impersonating Fury and the living dead.[59] At the climax of Statius' *Thebaid* the two human actors Polynices and Eteocles are, like Aeneas and Turnus, left alone on the battlefield as the supernatural actors withdraw. Jocasta stresses the fact that it is *themselves, ipsi* repeated twice at 11.330, instead of the 'delegation of crime' (11.332 *facinus mandasse parum est*). But this 'real presence' is itself a mark of alienation: the brothers meet each other in single combat only because they have become more Fury-like than the Furies themselves, who take on the role of passive spectators like Virgil's Latinus (11.537–8): 'No longer is there any need of the Furies; they simply marvel and stand on the sideline applauding, and they are distressed that human fury is more potent [than the Furies].' And in the Theban brothers the confusion and interchangeability of the two opponents naturally reaches its extreme.

[58] For the conflation of *Fama* and (epic) *fama* in the *Aeneid* see Hardie (1986), 275 n. 118.   [59] Pertinent remarks in Klinnert (1970), 104 ff.

Statius also explores alienation at the moment when the father Oedipus emerges from the shadows to embrace the bodies of his sons on the battlefield (11.580–633). His anger now turns to a *pietas* that is close to pity; he opens his speech with three abstractions who are also goddesses working on or in him: *Pietas, Clementia, Natura.* He regrets the curse he uttered whose workings he now sees before him, and refuses to believe that the words of the curse were really his (11.619–21): 'Those were the words of fury and Erinys, of the father and the mother, the kingdom and my lost eyes; I said nothing' *furor illa [uerba] et mouit Erinys|et pater et genetrix et regna oculique cadentes;|nil ego.*[60] The ellipse of the verb in *nil ego* yields a striking expression of self-annihilation. The last word of Oedipus' speech, 'father' *patrem,* (626 'now at least allow your father to come between you') points to a self-definition, but of course it is precisely in this word that the problems with Oedipus' identity lie. He had begun by talking of an internal division between his present feelings and his quality as father (607): 'Nature, ah, you conquer the wretched father!'

In Latin epic death cannot extinguish the vitality of the actors; they live on to demand blood offerings, or as reincarnations in the breasts of others, or in memory to delude with the appearance of presence – or to strut the stage in other epics. In the *Thebaid* the sap of this uncanny vitality rises highest in the funeral of Polynices and Eteocles in book 12. The rites of the funeral pyre should lay to rest, setting a clear demarcation between the worlds of the dead and the living, but the effect of the pious labour of Argia and Antigone is more akin to the criminal interference of Lucan's Erictho. When they come upon (what they cannot know to be) the dying embers of Eteocles' pyre, a small glow still lives (12.424 *aduiuere*), flame enough to fire the survival of the brothers after death.[61] 'The brothers have returned': 429 *ecce iterum fratres.* The divided fire of the pyre is the fulfilment of the fire-divination of Teiresias in book 10, a strange realization of an omen through reduplication of the phenomenon rather than through symbolic re-enactment. Yet there is a difference, in that the identical phenomenon conceals different realities: the flames of the pyromancy were signs of the brothers, whereas the flames of the pyre are in a sense the very substance of the living individuals. The simile at 433–4 provides a mythological gloss to this survival beyond the grave: the two flames are like torches of the Furies, those embodiments of the

---

[60] This goes far beyond the simple assignment of responsibility in the Homeric model, *Iliad* 19.86–7 (Agamemnon) 'I am not to blame, but Zeus and Moira and the Fury that walks in mist'. [61] See also p. 78 below.

undying anger of the dead. The horror is perhaps not so easy to define: Antigone uses imperfects in her redoubled exclamation 'this was my brother' *frater erat* (438–40), and reserves the present tense for line 441: 'their relentless hatred lives, it lives' *uiuunt odia improba, uiuunt*,[62] pointing to the alienation that replaced the natural bond of brotherhood to begin with. Even after the physical remains of Polynices have been consumed (455) the unnatural discord of the brothers reduplicates itself in the persons of Argia and Antigone disputing the claim to responsibility for the 'criminal' cremation in front of Creon's men; as the two women are separated by their pious discord, they also dismember the identity of Polynices (457–9): 'they compete, the one to snatch the body of her brother, the other the body of her husband, and take it in turns to prove their claims: "I brought the body" – "I the fire"; "I was led by piety" – "I by love".'[63]

The womenfolk of the Argive dead at Thebes look to a third city, Athens, for the vindication of the claims of Nature (12.561, 645). The status of the last book of the *Thebaid* is difficult: does it represent a satisfactory dismantling of the engines of civil war, or is it merely a perfunctory and unpersuasive cap? Within the terms of the present discussion a few points may be made. To start with, in contradistinction to the sacrificial orgies of Thebes, the Altar of Clemency in Athens at which the Argive women supplicate is emphatically not a place of sacrifice; on this altar of the human heart the only offerings are tears. Clemency 'delights in making the human mind and heart her habitation' (12.494), a kindly god of possession to keep out the squatting Fury, and a refuge from the 'anger, threats, and thrones' (504–5) of epic. In later times the Altar of Clemency 'overcame the fury of Oedipus and defended Orestes from his mother' (12.509–11): with this last example Statius hints at the supersession of the cycle of revenge at the end of the *Oresteia*, an ending that Virgil also reworks at the end of the *Aeneid*. But if this is a signal that the sacrificial resolution of crisis is to be superseded, it is disturbing to find that Theseus himself, in a replay of the last lines of the *Aeneid*, represents the death of Creon as a sacrifice (12.771–3): 'He thunders out: "Ghosts of Argos, here is a victim for you; open wide the jaws of Tartarus and get ready the avenging Eumenides, here comes Creon".' But any hope that this final act will really confine the operations

---

[62] Cf. 11.565–6 (the wounded Eteocles) 'fuelled with hatred the slender remains of his flickering life-force': the same hatred that will keep the feeble glow of the pyre alive.

[63] See Henderson (1991), 74–5 nn. 149–50. For the pious division of Polynices, cf. also the two women's joint lamentation at 12.385–90.

of the Furies to their torture chamber in Tartarus has already been undermined by the apparent possession of Theseus by the angry dead at 709–14: 'The Athenian general, meanwhile, when he saw the rays shine through the broken clouds and the sunlight on the front line of armour, leapt down into the field that still held the unburied ghosts under the walls; taking a deep breath through his dusty helmet of the air tainted with those hellish vapours he gave a groan and blazed out in a battle-flame of righteous anger.'

Statius has already been at work manipulating our image of Theseus. Three similes are applied to him: in the first (601–5) he is compared to a bull recently successful in defending his cows and pasture, and now preparing to fight again for the possession of yet another territory. The bull is *the* image for Polynices and Eteocles; is Theseus just another in that series of macho power-crazed warriors? But in the second simile (650–5) Theseus is like the storm-god Jupiter, in combinatorial imitation of beginning and end of the *Aeneid*, the storm in book 1 and the implicit equation of Aeneas and Jupiter at the close of book 12. This simile implies that the man Theseus has taken over the role of supreme arbiter that the real Jupiter had abrogated when he withdrew from the action at 11.134–5. In the third simile (733–5) Theseus is like Mars, a figure for the fury of war that presupposes no moral distinctions, but which we may note is modelled on a Virgilian simile applied to Turnus (*Aen.* 12.331–6). There is one more image of Theseus to be observed, in the ecphrasis of the Shield of Theseus described at 12.665–76. In Virgil Aeneas lifts a shield that bears images of his descendants, and in particular of Augustus of whom Aeneas is himself the 'type'; Theseus carries a picture of himself[64] (668 *seque ipsum*) wrestling with the Minotaur. This is an example both to others and to himself (12.672–6): 'He fills the nations with terror when he enters battle sheathed in this fierce image. Twice over do they look on Theseus, twice over on his hands bloody with killing; he himself remembers his past deeds when he beholds on the shield his band of companions, the threshold that once struck fear, and the Cretan girl growing pale as he paid out the clue.' The language of division[65] here applies to a king who is completely himself, whose present is continuous

---

[64] As also does Hannibal in Silius 2.426–8, 451–2.

[65] *Theb.* 12.673–4 *bis Thesea bisque cruentas│caede uidere manus* echo a paradigm of incompletion in *Aen.* 6.32–3 (the Cretan Daedalus' attempt to include a picture of his son in another ecphrasis) 'twice he tried to depict his fall in the gold, twice his father's hands fell from the work' *bis conatus erat casus effingere in auro,│bis patriae cecidere manus.*

and consistent with his past, and who derives the confidence to act from the memory of the past. Here at last, perhaps, is a self-sufficient epic 'man'.

However we assess the victory of Theseus, the epic ends not with triumph but with lament, or rather with the *praeteritio* of lament, a programme to inspire another epic (808 *nouus . . . furor*) to balance the programme at 1.33–45 for the epic we have actually read. The list of the dead attackers should extend to six, but after the first three (Capaneus, Tydeus, Polynices; leaving out Hippomedon and Amphiaraus), Statius' brevity is waylaid by the three-line expansion on the slightest of the Seven, Parthenopaeus, the point of stasis at which Statius takes his leave of his potentially endless subject-matter. It is a good moment to stop, for Virgil had also ended with a dead Arcadian, Pallas. But where the Virgilian Pallas had focused the final gathering of epic wrath, Parthenopaeus is the source of a grief that at last brings the two sides together (807): 'the Arcadian, whom the twin armies equally lamented' *Arcada, quem* geminae pariter *fleuere cohortes*. The name of his nationality is repeated three times in the same case at the beginning of three consecutive lines (805–7); in the final count the tripling of grief overbids the gemination of civil war,[66] where the doubling of the name of Pallas in Aeneas' final words seemed to point to the violence that arose out of differing claims on the dead boy and his goods. Grief for the Arcadian (temporarily) monopolizes the theatre of epic warfare. The spending of his blood immobilizes violence, as the dead ephebe is frozen eternally on the boundary between boyhood and manhood (806): 'he kept his looks, though his blood had been spent' *consumpto seruantem sanguine uultus*. Paradoxically this most unstable of epic characters, the 'girl–boy', whose 'maiden-face' (the two etymologies of Partheno–pai–os, Parthen–op–aios) is the sign of that wavering identity, is, perhaps, at the end of the epic alone privileged to remain true to that identity, such as it is. If *consumpto sanguine* hints at the common epic image of the killing of the virginal warrior as the shedding of blood in defloration, then this is a defloration that fixes for ever the transient liminal state rather than affording a passage from virginity to adulthood.[67]

---

[66] The threefold repetition has its correlate in the ritual practice of calling for the last time on the dead thrice (*Od.* 9.64–5; *Aen.* 6.506), or of saying *uale uale uale* (compare the use of *ualete* to mark the end of a Roman comedy).

[67] The transience of the beauty of the *eromenos*, of which the beardless face is the mark, is an obsessive theme of Greek epigram: see Taran (1985); the passage of boyhood

Sacrifice and substitution 2

Cato's speech in book 2 of the *Bellum Ciuile* owes not a little to a speech in the *Aeneid* that is at first sight a surprising *locus* for the theme of sacrificial substitution, the lament of the mother of Euryalus at *Aeneid* 9.481–97.[68] Cato compares his grief at Rome's self-destruction to that of a father at the funeral of his sons; the mother of Euryalus bewails her inability to escort her son's funeral in due manner. Cato takes on the role of the *unus homo*; Euryalus' companion Nisus had earlier commented on the singular devotion of Euryalus' mother (*Aen.* 9.217–18): 'Alone of many mothers she was bold enough to follow you.' In her despair she calls out to the Italians to single her out as the target of their weapons (9.493–4): 'If you have any feeling, shoot me, hurl all your weapons at me, Rutulians, me first kill with your steel' *figite me, si qua est pietas, in me omnia tela|conicite, o Rutuli, me primam absumite ferro*. This is the model for Cato's 'attack me alone with your steel, me . . .' me *solum inuadite* ferro|me . . . (*Bell. Ciu.* 2.315–16). Euryalus' mother is in fact entirely selfish in her desire for death; her cry is a plea for other hands to carry out her suicide for her; the one person in whom her being is founded is now past the point where she could offer herself as a surrogate victim. But her words (and thus those of Cato) do enter a chain of substitution that leads back to the real possibility of self-sacrifice for another; unwittingly she echoes the words of Nisus when Volcens is about to kill Euryalus, at *Aeneid* 9.427–8: 'Me, me, here I am who did the deed, on me turn your weapons, Rutulians' *me, me, adsum qui feci, in me conuertite ferrum,|o Rutuli!* Nisus' self-revelation is in turn prompted by Volcens' intention to make of Euryalus a substitute victim for the unseen killer of two of his own men (422–3): 'But in the meanwhile you will pay me with your blood the penalty for both men.' When Volcens ignores his plea, Nisus' reaction to the killing of his friend is to take a life for a life, that of Volcens for that of Euryalus, and in so doing to bring about the

---

beauty may be described as a 'death'. Of Parthenopaeus Statius writes at 9.703–6 'not yet had his cheeks suffered the change of rosy down. He takes no delight in the praises of his beauty, and strains to put on rough and sternly threatening looks, but a becoming anger preserves his good looks' (*sed frontis* seruat *honorem|ira decens*). His death has the same effect as castration: *Silu.* 3.4.65–6 (Aesculapius castrates Earinus) 'so that the first down should not pluck the brightness from his cheeks and the charm of his fair beauty suffer eclipse'. On killing virgins, see Fowler (1987).

[68] Also the model for Cornelia's outburst on the death of Pompey at 8.639 ff.

49

self-immolation for which he had earlier called. The language fore-shadows Turnus' singling-out of Pallas;[69] but the motivation and the emotion prefigure more closely the death that repays that choice of target, the killing of Turnus himself by Aeneas.[70] In the death of Nisus differences between both enemies and friends are equalized: firstly in the shared death of slayer and slain (9.443 'as he died he robbed his enemy of his life', of which the Statian deaths of Polynices and Eteocles may be read as a grimmer variant); and secondly in the union in death of the two lovers (444–5 'then pierced full of holes he threw himself on top of his lifeless friend'). The extraordinary benediction that Virgil bestows on the 'two happy youths' (9.446) who consummate their love in death perhaps gains some of its force through contrast with the grim loneliness of Aeneas at the end of the poem, survivor to both his friend and his enemy.[71]

Silius also alludes to the mother of Euryalus in an extended series of sacrificial substitutions. Hannibal derives his power from a sacrificial encounter with the shade of Dido (1.81–122).[72] In the *Punica* the sacrificial image of slaughter on the battlefield is common; a particularly close network of allusion is woven around the battle of Lake Trasimene narrated in *Punica* 5. At 4.735 Juno appearing in a dream to Hannibal promises him a victory in which 'you will sate with slaughter your father's shade'. Hannibal is almost immediately called on to make another kind of sacrifice, that of his own son as the annual child-sacrifice at Carthage (4.763–73: an institution founded by Dido herself). We slide through a series of substitutions, and Hannibal, given the unprecedented privilege of choosing whether or not to comply with the lot, manipulates the process of substitution in order to divert the sacrificial violence from his son on to the enemy (4.822 'for I am preparing a sacrifice and building greater altars', namely the anticipated Roman dead at Trasimene).

[69] With *Aen.* 9.438–9 'But Nisus rushes into their midst and attacks Volcens alone among the many, he has time for Volcens alone' *at Nisus ruit in medios solumque per omnis\Volcentem petit, in solo Volcente moratur*, compare 10.442–3 'I alone am matched with Pallas, Pallas is owed to me alone' *solus ego in Pallanta feror, soli mihi Pallas\debetur*.

[70] Cf. also 9.443 *condidit* with 12.950 *condit*; 442 *fulmineum* looks forward to Aeneas' fulmineous spear-throw at 12.919–26.

[71] The devotion of Nisus and Euryalus finds a further parallel in Brutus' hero-worship of Cato; their fervent and pious nocturnal deliberation, like that of Virgil's two young Trojans, issues in a laudable but excessive resolve at 2.324–5, with which compare the language of *Aen.* 9.182, 354.   [72] See pp. 64–5 below.

Sacrificial substitution intersects with, and threatens to annihilate, generational replacement.[73] Hannibal sees his son not as the one sacrificial victim but as the 'one hope' (4.815; cf. 3.69–96) of his family and of Carthage. In him he recognizes himself (3.75–6): 'I recognize your father's face and the eyes glowering under that fierce brow.' The boy's mother Imilce echoes the language of Nisus and the mother of Euryalus in offering herself as a substitute sacrifice (4.798) 'Me, me, who bore him, kill in payment of your vows' *me, me, quae genui, uestris absumite uotis.*

A part of Hannibal's wishes is granted, a part is withheld. His decision to substitute hosts of Roman victims for his one son is successfully carried through at Trasimene. The benighted Flaminius attempts to define Hannibal as the scapegoat–victim (5.153): 'this one life will be payment enough for all our dead' *unum hoc pro cunctis sat erit caput*; his desire to parade the Punic general's head on a pike for parents to gaze on in revengeful satisfaction is an inversion of the parading of the heads of Euryalus and Nisus before the Trojan camp and the mother of Euryalus in *Aeneid* 9.471–2. In the end it is the Gallic Ducarius who offers up the life (*caput*) of Flaminius as a sacrificial offering to the shades of the Boii triumphed over earlier by Flaminius (5.652–3): 'My countrymen, feel no regret in sacrificing this life to our brave ghosts.' But on the other hand Hannibal's hopes that his son will take his place as great leader of his people (4.818 'apply yourself to my task') will come to nothing.[74]

Nisus and Euryalus had been caught up in sacrificial patterns from their first appearance in the *Aeneid*.[75] In the foot-race in *Aeneid* 5, which

---

[73] See p. 96 below.

[74] For a commentary, see *Pun.* 15.463–6, where Laelius gives the gods their due by killing the Carthaginian Gala whose mother had saved him from child-sacrifice by secretly substituting another victim. For similarly thwarted attempts by the Carthaginians to elude the demands of their own sacrificial practice, see Diod. Sic. 20.14. At the end of the same book, after the battle of Metaurus, it is the head of Hasdrubal that is paraded before his brother Hannibal; Nero makes the point about substitution (814–16): 'With your brother's head we have repaid you, Hannibal, for Cannae, Trebia and Trasimene', this provokes sacrificial thoughts from Hannibal (820–1): 'He muttered with closed lips that in time he would make worthy offerings to his brother's shade.'

[75] Putnam (1965), ch. 2 'Games and Reality' discusses the links in book 5 between the sacrificial aspects of the funeral games and the 'sacrifice' of Palinurus at the end of the book, but in the service of a piously moralizing message (p. 65): 'the necessity of sacrifice through suffering, sometimes even self-sacrifice, to reach for . . . the goals of heroism'. Sansone (1988) theorizes on the sacrificial origins of sport; see esp. 80–6 on the fillet worn by victorious athletes as well as by sacrificial victims and priests.

anticipates many of the motifs of their more serious business in book 9,
Nisus slips in the blood and dung of sacrificed cattle in the very moment
of victory (5.331), but has the presence of mind to trip the runner-up in
order to allow Euryalus the victory. In this accident Nisus falls down flat
like the sacrificial victim (332–3 *pronus . . . concidit*),[76] but is able to effect
the required substitution for himself. The games are a sacrificial
occasion, offered to the spirit of Anchises; in the foot-race the sacrificial
frame and sporting event are unfortunately confused: there is blood on
the track. There is a risk of a similar confusion in the next contest, the
boxing-match. One of the fighters, Dares, had killed a man in a match at
the tomb of Hector (5.371–4), a detail which reminds us of the actual
origin of Roman gladiatorial *munera*; his victim, Butes, was a Bebrycian,
a subject of Amycus, a boxer notorious for challenging and killing
strangers as sacrifices to Neptune.[77] Aeneas stops the match when
Entellus is in danger of inflicting mortal injuries on Dares, and Entellus
takes the prize, a bull, which he immediately sacrifices to his dead master
Eryx as a substitute for Dares (474–6): 'See from what a death you have
saved Dares.' The *caestus*, instrument of sport, becomes the sacrificial
instrument, but the potential confusion between sport and the real
thing[78] is clarified through sacrificial substitution (483–4): 'This life I pay
you, Eryx, as a better offering instead of the death of Dares; here in
victory I lay down my gloves and my profession.' A contest and a career
end with sacrifice. The games are bounded by ritual sacrifice, but the
violence threatens to spill over into the sport; this confusion of framing
and framed events is realized at the very end of the poem where, as we
have seen, the boundary between the sacrifice that ratifies the *foedus* in
book 12 and the violence of the duel that is thereby sanctioned is
overstepped.[79]

Euryalus' cry *me, me* and his mother's unwitting echo proliferate in

---

[76] *OLD concido* 1c 'poet. of victims', as at Lucr. 1.98–9 of Iphianassa 'collapsing as
victim in the moment of her wedding' (likewise a sudden reversal of a moment of
joy).

[77] The sacrificial aspects are stressed in Valerius Flaccus' account of Amycus, whose
victims in boxing are compared (*Argon.* 4.151–3) to bulls at the altar. At 337–43
Pollux's victory is sealed with a proper sacrifice.

[78] Classically at *Iliad* 22.159–61 'they were not competing for a sacrificial victim or an
oxhide, which are the prizes men win in the foot-race, but they were running for the
life of Hector', imitated at *Aen.* 12.764–5. Cf. Silius *Pun.* 16.527–48; Stat. *Theb.*
6.911–14.

[79] Note also the disturbing enthusiasm of the rowers at 5.230 'they are willing to barter
their lives for glory' *uitamque uolunt* pro laude *pacisci*, echoed in Turnus' words at
12.49 'allow me to barter death for glory' *letumque sinas pro laude pacisci*.

later epics down to the Renaissance. The Virgin's lament at the cross in both Vida's *Christiad*, 5.850–8, and Sannazaro's *De Partu Virginis*, 1.344–67 draws on the lament of the mother of Euryalus. In Milton's *Paradise Lost* the repetition of 'me' repeatedly provides a focus for that poem's thematization of Christian sacrificial substitution and ties together Christ, Adam and Satan in a plot of altruism and selfishness. The Virgilian echo is found first in Christ's intervention to define the central fact of redemption at 3.236–8

> Behold me then, me for him, life for life
> I offer, on me let thine anger fall;
> Account me man . . .

It is used to justify Christ's claim to stand alone against the rebel angels at 6.809–23; the geminated 'me' is made the basis of a falsely conceived substitution in Satan's

> True is, me also he hath judged, or rather
> Me not, but the brute serpent in whose shape
> Man I deceived (10.494–6),

finally to appear as the vehicle for the contrite Adam's recognition of the true state of affairs at 10.737–41 and 10.831–3

> . . . first and last
> On me, me only, as the source and spring
> Of all corruption, all the blame lights due.[80]

Substitution thwarted

Slaughter in Lucan's *Bellum Ciuile* is routinely sacrificial: words like *macto, iugulo (iugulum)* pepper the text, suggesting the perversion of civilization that is civil war. In Lucan's inverted sacrifices there is both excess and deficiency: alongside the orgies of killing we also find the phenomenon of thwarted sacrificial substitution. For example the other-directed sacrifice of *deuotio* is rendered futile or self-destructive. The Pompeians at Ilerda, starving, rush desperately against the Caesarian line, 'devoted to certain death' (4.272). Caesar refuses them the gratification of dying on his men's swords, recognizing that this would indeed involve him in heavy loss (276–7): 'Here are men who hate life and hold themselves cheap, ready to perish at my cost.' Later in the same book the Caesarian Vulteius determines to inflict another paradoxical

---

[80] On other repetitions of 'me' in structures of vicariousness in *Paradise Lost*, see Shoaf (1985), ch. 3.

damnum (4.514) on his own general Caesar through a perversion of *deuotio* (533–4). But self-sacrifice is here literal suicide, and the death of the leader is not a substitute, but the model, for the immolation of all of his men, as Vulteius bares his throat for the sacrificial stroke (540–1). The 'virtuous' self-sacrifice of Vulteius and his men before the wondering eyes of the Pompeian spectators forms a 'gladiatorial' pair with the final episode of the book, the 'sacrifice' to the African ghosts of Curio and his men.

When Caesar braves the storm in book 5 he exposes himself to the elements as an *unum caput* that is *not* taken as an offering. His own men chide him for his rashness (5.685–7): 'When the life and security of so many peoples depend on this one life, and the great world has made this man its head, the wish for death is a cruelty'; but there are other points of view. At 6.305–13 we hear of the battle at Dyrrachium that does not take place, and which would have taken the place of all subsequent civil war battles. Similar is Statius' comment on the near-death of Polynices in the chariot race at *Thebaid* 6.513–17: 'What an opportunity for death, Theban, had cruel Tisiphone not denied you, how great a war you could have prevented. Thebe and your brother would have publicly mourned you, Argos and Nemea would have mourned you, Lerna and Larissa would have made you humble offerings of shorn locks, and you would have received greater honours than the tomb of Archemorus.' Polynices would have been an offering *in place of* the coming war, as the boundary between game and war was confused in the accidental death, resulting in a funeral of a participant in the funeral games of Archemorus, a 'victim' at the tomb. In that case we would not have had to wait for another six books for the lament that closes the epic.[81]

At Pharsalia, the decisive battle that yet fails to bring an end to civil war, the logic of the surrogate victim is given a number of twists. At 7.117–19 Pompey longs to be singled out: 'I could wish that the first spear of this funereal war might strike this head of mine, if my fall did not affect the outcome and involve the downfall of my party.' But here his wish, like that of the mother of Euryalus, is for a purely private gratification, so long as it does not prejudice the chances of his army; there is no sense of his own death as a saving sacrifice for the lives of his men. Pompey had begun his speech in reply to Cicero at 87–8 with the choice of the role of private soldier (one among many) rather than that of general (one for all).[82] At the end of the battle the one man identifies with his troops, but

---

[81] Compare the threefold *te* with the threefold *Arcada* of 12.805–7 (see p. 48 above).

[82] For the play on *dux*/*miles*, see p. 7 above.

as survivor with the dying, a precise inversion of the scapegoating that Cato wished for (652–3): 'He saw that all these weapons were aimed at his life, he saw all the corpses and himself perishing in that sea of blood.'

Caesar, like Pompey, uses the rhetoric (or plays the role, claims the costume) of being just one among many rather than the one leader (264–8): 'It's not my position that is at stake, but my prayer is for you the crowd, that you may gain your freedom by winning power over all peoples. I myself am eager to return to private life and play the part of a modest citizen in the common toga (*plebeiaque toga modicum componere ciuem*). In order that all things may be possible for you, there is no role that I refuse' (*omnia dum uobis liceant, nihil esse recuso*); (308–10) 'My concern is for you; for the prospect of a fate inflicted by my own hand frees me from concern for myself. The man who looks back before the enemy are beaten will see me stabbing my own entrails.'

> uestri cura mouet; nam me secura manebit
> sors quaesita manu: fodientem uiscera cernet
> me mea qui nondum uicto respexerit hoste.

Caesar like Pompey looks for (or pretends to) the release of a private death, but the image of the all-powerful Caesar turning his hand on himself (309–10 *fodientem uiscera . . . me mea*) demands to be read against the second and third lines of the poem, 'a powerful people turning its right hand against its own entrails' *in sua uictrici conuersum uiscera dextra*.[83] After this Caesar uses the logic of the arbitrary sacrificial victim, but as an argument for total slaughter rather than for the victimization of the one for the survival of the many (324–5): 'Even if a soldier's stroke violates no tie of blood, let him still claim credit for smiting this unknown enemy's throat as if it were a crime.'[84] *All* are to be slaughtered, all are to be singled out as victims. Pompey, on the other hand, in his speech to his troops vainly tries to turn the language of sacrificial bloodshed in his own favour (349–51): 'The better cause encourages us to hope for the favour of the gods: they themselves will guide our weapons through the entrails of Caesar, they themselves will wish to ratify the constitution of Rome with that blood.'[85] Brutus is present at Pharsalia, but is debarred by fate from taking Caesar as his victim until there is no possibility of sacrificing

---

[83] Cf. the figurative *uiscera* of Rome assaulted by Caesar later in the battle, 7.579, 722.

[84] I follow the interpretation of Housman and Postgate.

[85] Cf. also 9.1020–1; 10.371–2; Cic. *Sest.* 24 'they said that the treaty could be sealed and signed in my blood' *foedus meo sanguine ictum sanciri posse dicebant*; *red. Quir.* 13. Normally *foedera* were ratified with the blood of a pig.

him to save the generality (592–6): 'You achieve nothing there by aiming at Caesar's throat; he has not yet reached the peak of power, climbing higher than the summit of human law to which all things are subject, and so earned from fate the right to so noble a death. Let him live, and, that he may fall as Brutus' victim, let him be king' (*uiuat et, ut Bruti procumbat* uictima, *regnet*). But the juxtaposition of the last two words does reveal another logic, that of the king who must die.

Pharsalia, then, is a tale of missed opportunities, in which the ultimate orgy of violence of a sacrificial crisis still fails to spend itself. Pompey's sacrifice before battle fails in a conventional way, when the bull escapes from the altar and (7.167) 'no victim was found for the funereal sacrifice'. But the omen has perhaps a further significance: at the funeral rites of Rome celebrated at Pharsalia there was no victim whose death could bring an end to the indiscriminate series of civil strife. Pompey might seem to be the natural victim, but, like the bull, he flies from the scene of sacrifice (8.1–5). The point at which the epic breaks off is curiously suggestive of an ending just beyond the last line. Achillas has been killed, a 'victim' offered to the shade of Magnus; we have already seen how this man, both by his name and by his actions, is a narrative surrogate for Caesar. The poem has now turned into an epic of revenge that will not reach its end until the final victim, Caesar, has been offered. Lucan specifies that that revenge will be (and by poetic justice must be) achieved by the swords of Caesar's fatherland (10.528–9); but the immediate situation offers the possibility of a substitute, and premature, enactment of that revenge, by the swords of the Egyptians (532–3): 'By that moment of supreme crisis for Caesar this one day could have gone down in history' *potuit discrimine summo|Caesaris una dies in famam et saecula mitti*. The scales are in the balance, as when Jupiter weighed the fates of Aeneas and Turnus, and we are left hanging in mid-air.[86] In hindsight we know that history missed that opportunity also.

[86] Note also the bravura of Pothinus at 10.385–94 with its suggestion of an ending like that of the *Aeneid:* 'Behold, here comes a more famous victim . . . This night will complete the business of civil war and provide an offering for the peoples that have perished, and send down to the shades the life that is still owed to the world. Steel your hearts, go for the throat of Caesar.'

3

Heaven and Hell

Virgil transforms the epic's traditional concern with power and the wielders of power by making the stage for the struggle for power nothing less than the universe itself. In doing this he was exactly in tune with the ideological consciousness of the Romans, and was a determining voice in the crystallization of that consciousness. The idea that Rome was destined to be the ruler of the world had begun with an awareness of the significance of the Second Punic War;[1] it had then fuelled the competing claims to power of the warring dynasts of the late Republic, to become the inheritance of the sole *princeps*, who could shield himself against the danger of the renewed division and disintegration of the state only through the fiction that in his one person, *unus*, he embodied the whole, *omnes* or *omnia*.

Virgil's canny identification of the *Roman* centre of the epic ensured that the genre had a vigorous after-life; through the transposition of the theme of universal power from the terrestrial to the celestial plane the Virgilian epic easily became the Christian epic. The Biblical story, as told for example in the epics of Vida and Milton, has as its plot-line 'the world destroyed and world restored', in which the Incarnation makes of the universal god a man who is also all men, another scapegoat who takes the sins of the world upon his head. The Christian epic tells of a universal struggle of a particular sort, that between the forces of Heaven and Hell. But in this respect too the necessary adjustment had already been made by Virgil. So far as we can tell, in the absence of so much earlier

---

[1] This is important for Silius' choice of theme: the Second Punic War is not just the time when Rome showed her greatest moral and political strength, but also the point at which the theme of universal power enters history in the here-and-now rather than in prospect (as in the *Aeneid*).

Hellenistic and Roman epic,[2] the *Aeneid* innovates by the introduction of a radical dualism into the epic conflict, a dualism which then enters the Roman tradition to flow in an uninterrupted stream into the Christian successors (the polymorphous *Metamorphoses* is an exception in resisting this dualism, though it is not immune to the influence of the *Aeneid*).

The whale-bone stiffening of the epic plot with a rigidly dualistic scheme of the order of things might seem to lead only to an unwelcome simplification and abstraction of the genre. But Virgil's remarkable powers are one step ahead of themselves: Virgil's dualistic scheme already contains its own contradictions and tensions of such a kind that final stability is never attained. It is this built-in instability that makes the *Aeneid* a perpetually mobile text which invites ever new interpretations, whether in the form of scholarly commentary or of further epic rewritings of the story. The spatial fluidity of the boundary between Heaven and Hell finds a temporal analogue in history as the Romans try at the succession of each new emperor to make *this* the definitive version of the Augustan settlement, the final return of the Golden Age, a dream of stability that never loses its potency at each new plunge into the maelstrom of history.

Heaven and Hell in the *Aeneid*: the basic scheme

The dualism of the *Aeneid* is well enough known (though it is perhaps not always thought of as such), as is also the instability, whose sign is the unending attempts of critics to decide whether Virgil intends us to approve or disapprove of Aeneas and his descendant Augustus. The basic dualism is most often expressed through moral and psychological abstractions, above all *pietas* and *furor*, or reason and unreason. This kind of dualism may be accommodated within a monistic Stoicism; less comfortable is a theological dualism that constantly hovers on the edge of a full-blown Manichaeism: the poem becomes a conflict between powers of the upper and lower worlds, between the forces of light and dark. Relations within the Olympian family are threatened by this dualism, with the supreme female, Juno, operating through subterranean and chthonic forces (the Gigantomachic winds, Allecto), and the supreme male, Jupiter, firmly placed at the zenith, and operating through Mercury, the Italian version of Hermes, a god of the word and of reason.

---

[2] The possible presence of Gigantomachic imagery in Hellenistic historical epic would be one place to look for dualism: see Hardie (1986) 125–43.

In Greco–Roman religion the traditional area for a sharply defined dualism is the Underworld, divided between the dark Tartarus, the place of the sinners, and bright Elysium, the place of the blessed; in the *Aeneid* this division is vividly described in book 6, but it is also projected on to the world above, where there is an alternation between places and times evocative of the Elysian Fields (or of its close relative, the landscape of the Golden Age) and waking Hells. 'Hell on Earth' becomes one of the most obsessive motifs of the later epic; the projection of eschatological states into the here-and-now also seems to correspond at a deep level to the Romans' experience of their history in the first century A.D.

As well as describing a *struggle* between forces of good and evil, the *Aeneid* also traces a *journey* from Hell to Heaven. Troy is a 'world destroyed', but in its hour of destruction it is cruelly transformed into a version of the Underworld, a Hellish nocturne (another example of the projection of the next world on to this).[3] Aeneas' journey is to an Italy described in terms of the Lucretian abode of the gods (1.205 *sedes quietas*), or of an Elysian idyll (7.25–36). Within the span of the text itself, our reading takes us from the dominance of an infuriated and Hellish Juno (the storm in book 1) to the victory of the sky-god Jupiter over the agents of Juno and Allecto. This progress from Hell to Heaven was naturally imitated in the Christian epic (e.g. Dante and Milton), but it may also be traced in the pagan epics of the first century A.D. The *Metamorphoses* describes a temporal path from creation to the poet's own day; but the starting-point, Chaos, is also a version of the Underworld,[4] and the poem ends with the translation of Caesar – and Ovid – to the stars. Lucan's *Bellum Ciuile* begins at night with characters figuratively out of the Underworld; we do not know how it would have ended, but this epic at least could hardly have concluded with a straight-faced version of a Roman paradise. The reader has to decide how straight a face to keep when in the proem he reads of the ultimate justification of the Hell of civil war in the coming of Nero, the Jupiter on earth who will in good time take his place in Heaven. Statius begins the *Thebaid* with repeated eruptions from Hades; the chain of crime is broken by the intervention of the godlike Theseus, just ruler of Athens, a city loved by the gods. In Valerius Flaccus' *Argonautica* chaos and Hell

---

[3] With the shadows of Troy, 2.420 *obscura nocte per umbram*, compare the descent of Aeneas and the Sibyl into the Underworld, 6.268 *ibant obscuri sola sub nocte per umbram*. On this and other parallels between Troy and the Underworld, see Putnam (1965), 30–48.   [4] *OLD chaos* 2 'The underworld'. Cf. Chambers (1963), 66.

figure largely in the first book, though not at the very beginning; the end of the poem is missing, but the four-line proem takes the story up to the catasterism of the *Argo* (which, it may be noted, was not the ending of Apollonius of Rhodes' *Argonautica*). Silius gets us going with the Hellish Hannibal; the first major episode is the siege of Saguntum, where Hell comes up into this world (as in the Virgilian model, the Sack of Troy in *Aeneid* 2). The *Punica* ends with the triumph of the godlike Scipio and the procession up to the Capitol, the Roman height where god meets man. This corresponds to the final scene on the Shield of Aeneas in *Aeneid* 8, the triumph of the man Augustus staged before the temple of the sun-god Apollo; but the stress in Silius on Jupiter points also to the finale of *Aeneid* 12. The last word of the *Punica* is *Tonantis*, '(Jupiter) the thunderer', the supreme Olympian in his manifestation as the angry god, the god who lends the force of the thunderbolt to Aeneas' final spear-throw against Turnus.

The energy of Hell

The use of Hell as a starting-point is more than the mark of conformity to a convenient and obvious story pattern. It also seems to symbolize the burst of power needed both by the actors and the narrator to provide the momentum for a long poem, and a long poem that might be in danger of an inability to escape the gravitational pull of its many predecessors. Of the two states of Heaven and Hell, Hell is the source of the greater energy. Heaven is stasis, peace, rest; Hell ceaseless movement, war, emotional turmoil. Hell is the more invasive, the more disruptive of equilibrium; Hell is likely to be the starting-point of a new movement. With this in mind let us return to take a second look at the beginnings of epics.

The pattern is established with the storm at the beginning of the *Aeneid*, an afflatus that is released from Hell to fill the sails of the epic, for the winds of Aeolus are nature-spirits of a Titanic or Gigantic kind.[5] Repeated outbursts through the poem ensure that momentum is maintained, crucially at the beginning of the second half of the poem when a state of equilibrium threatens. Ovid's *Metamorphoses* begins with Chaos, of which the Underworld is the continuing image, a state of war and perpetual changefulness (1.17 'nothing kept its shape' *nulli sua forma manebat*) on which the 'god and a better nature' (21) impose order and

---

[5] Hardie (1986) ch. 3.

peace; in Virgilian terms the act of creation represents the stability that is the epic's goal, and which in this epic seems to have been reached when we are scarcely under way. The rest of the poem is an account of the transformations that continually dissolve the god's perfect handiwork; a poem on change has a vested interest in the repetition of chaos, in things that do not keep their shape. Or rather, things and persons pass through a moment of 'chaos' from which they emerge in a new permanency that represents the order of the poet rather than the order of the original demiurge.

Lucan's epic begins at night and with Caesar's vision of the goddess Roma, proleptically and by literary descent already an inhabitant of the Underworld, for she is modelled on the ghost of Hector which appears to Aeneas on the night of the Sack of Troy to warn him that the city is already lost and that he must set out on a journey to find a new city. This is the second beginning of the *Aeneid* in order of books, but the first in absolute chronology, and inverts the themes of the uprising of the winds. Here is another initiative from the Underworld, but this time from a benevolent spirit, and one who represents the powerlessness of the past and in effect issues a challenge to continue a tradition that has run out of steam. (In the storm in book 1 it is Aeneas who lacks all power.) The diminished force of the once energetic Hector meets resistance from Aeneas, who finds other, apparently internal, sources of energy that impel him to do the opposite of what Hector urges, in a fury that threatens prematurely to destroy the epic's course: had Aeneas died at Troy, as he desires (*Aen.* 2.317), the energy of the epic would have been dissipated for lack of a hero. In Lucan the figure from the other side, the personified Roma, is similarly powerless, confronting a living human who incorporates the forces of Hell (the reader cannot escape the irony of 1.200–1 'I do not pursue you with the Furies' weapons' *non te furialibus armis\persequor*). Caesar's crossing of the Rubicon will make of Italy a Hell on Earth.

Caesar is both an anti-Aeneas and a Turnus: in the *Aeneid* Aeneas' vision of the ghost of Hector is repeated and parodied in the appearance of Allecto to Turnus in 7, an episode that sets Turnus on his course to destruction and that gets the epic going again with a fresh blast from Hell after a journey through the Underworld in the previous book that had seemed to fix everything in a timeless vision of the Roman order. The intervention of Allecto is a re-enactment *both* of the storm in book 1 *and* of the vision of Hector in book 2. The female figure who appears to

Lucan's Caesar is herself an anti-Allecto, attempting to stand up for the continuity of Rome whereas Allecto attempts to disrupt by violent transformation of the *status quo*. Caesar is the representative of the Furies. In the simile at 1.205–12 he is compared to an African lion working himself up into a frenzy of anger: the model is the simile comparing Turnus to a wounded lion in the Carthaginian fields at *Aeneid* 12.4–8, near the end of Turnus' career of Hellishly inspired violence (the simile also pairs Turnus with Hannibal as public enemies of Rome). In another example of the epic's tendency to make endings into beginnings,[6] Caesar at the outset of his epic action plays Turnus at the end. The self-motivation of Caesar in contrast to Turnus' manipulation from outside is brought out in the detail of the lion lashing himself into a state of anger with his tail, where it had taken the snaky lash of Allecto to overcome Turnus' reluctance (*Aen.* 7.451). Caesar is in truth not really so autonomous as he seems: his part has already been acted out by Turnus and Hannibal, he too is possessed by the spirits of others. This scene suggests by allusion and irony that his energy derives from Hell. Further, Caesar in himself embodies the confusion of Heaven and Hell that we shall shortly examine; in a simile at 1.151–7 his demonic energy had been compared to that of a thunderbolt, the instrument of Jupiter's anger. Here it is a thunderbolt that falls on Jupiter's own temples of Jupiter (155) in an indiscriminate exercise of celestial force.

The Allecto episode in *Aeneid* 7 is one of the passages most frequently imitated in post-Virgilian epic; it doubtless fulfils all the 'Silver' requirements for horror, violent emotion, hyperbole, but it also performs important thematic and structural functions. Nowhere is it used more insistently than in Statius' *Thebaid*, a twelve-book epic on civil war which in a sense starts with book 7 of the *Aeneid*, omitting the Odyssean wandering of *Aeneid* 1–6 (although Statius finds other ways to delay the final battle that expends, temporarily, the epic's energy). The action begins in book 1 with the figure of Oedipus, like Virgil's Hector and Lucan's Roma a figure from the past who transmits duties and injunctions to the future. Here the powerless old man is, paradoxically, as potent as Allecto (who had disguised herself as a weak old woman in her first approach to Turnus); like Milton's Satan, Oedipus is a creature of light who has fallen into a pit of darkness, alienated from sources of power within both family and state (Oedipus is no longer the king, and

---

his paternal position has been invalidated). But Statius uses the tragic figure of the king made scapegoat as the source of energy for his epic. Oedipus has condemned himself to an eternal darkness, to a living 'death' (1.48). That is to say he has chosen to make for himself an Underworld in this world,[7] despite 'the cruel daylight in his mind' (52). Oedipus is to make of himself an agent of possession, but he himself is a man possessed by 'the Furies of his crimes in his breast' (52), those Furies that have been fuelling the epic ever since the *Aeneid*. Incensed at the failure of his sons to pay attention to him (which might be interpreted as their doomed attempt to make a clean break with the past), he calls on Tisiphone to exact vengeance on them, which she does by exciting strife between the brothers. Their inability to escape the repetition of crime imposed by the tragic curse consigns the poet, Statius, to a repetition of the Virgilian epic plot.

Statius' procedure in his other, fragmentary, epic, the *Achilleid*, is interestingly different. In the *Thebaid* Statius chooses not to tell the whole story of Thebes, the 'long chain stretching back' *longa retro series* (1.7); in the *Achilleid* he justifies his presumptuous choice of Homer's own hero by including those things that Homer does not narrate, i.e. the whole life of Achilles.[8] This more leisurely kind of epic dispenses with the violent beginnings that we have examined so far, but not without making it clear that this is a deliberate choice. We begin as Paris' ship sets sail from Sparta, Helen the cargo. Thetis, in the foreknowledge of the consequences of the rape for her son, considers destroying Paris now. This is the role of Juno at the beginning of the *Aeneid*, but here Thetis is diverted from her plan by Neptune, who consoles her with the thought of the glory that Achilles will win in the war fought over Helen. The epic storm that does not take place, so far from unleashing the energy necessary to set the poem in motion, would in fact have made it impotent in removing the material of the hero's martial exploits. Neptune tells Thetis that he will allow her her storm on the return of the Greeks from Troy, when together they will work out their grudges against Ulysses. The storm at Cape Caphareus is the same one that Juno appeals to as

---

[7] For this liminal state, see Sen. *Oed.* 949–51 'Choose a drawn-out death. Look for a path where you may wander apart from the buried yet banished from the living.'

[8] In *Theb.* 1.7–15 (the material that he will not treat) Statius summarizes Ovid *Met.* 3 and 4; by his use of the Ovidian *deducere* (*Met.* 1.4) at *Ach.* 1.7 'to lead the youth through the whole story of Troy' *tota iuuenem deducere Troia*, Statius signals that this epic will be an Ovidian 'continuous song' *perpetuum carmen.*

precedent for her plan for vengeance in *Aeneid* 1; thus Statius puts us in mind of the epic beginning that he does *not* use.

The connection between the energy of Hell and the power needed to get the epic under way is seen most clearly at the beginning of Silius' *Punica*, which like Statius' *Achilleid* tells of the childhood of its main actor, but not here in a rustic idyll guided by a humanized Centaur. Hannibal is a hero in the mould of Lucan's Caesar, but this thunderbolt of demonic energy also turns out to be a vehicle for other beings. He 'puts on (*induit*) all the anger of Juno' (1.38), as if he were a mannikin to be clothed by the goddess. This is also a way of saying that he takes on a Virgilian role, for the anger of Juno is of course the divine wrath that energizes the *Aeneid*.[9] The immediate channel for Juno's anger in the *Punica* is not a storm but the spirit of Juno's human favourite and instrument in the *Aeneid*, Dido. The shrine of Dido, at the centre of the city and on the spot where she killed herself in Virgil, an enlargement of the shrine of Sychaeus in Dido's palace at *Aeneid* 4.457–9, is the gateway to Hell in this epic. The ancestor figure Dido, like Statius' Oedipus, is present and not present, alive and not alive,[10] in the form of a motionless statue that sweats at the moment of the successful evocation of the ghosts of the dead (including, we may presume, the shade of Dido herself). The point of all this is, of course, to activate the words of Dido's curse at *Aeneid* 4.625 'arise, someone, as avenger from my bones'; in his oath the boy Hannibal unwittingly uses the words of Virgil's Dido.[11] Silius lays bare in a particularly obvious way the close association in imperial epic between the generation of narrative themes through an outburst of the forces of the Underworld and the generation of a new epic by reversion to the model of the *Aeneid*, animating the *Aeneid's* own allusions to the afterlife of its characters.[12] In the case of Silius life and literature interact in a curious way: Pliny the Younger tells us of his devotion to the memory of Virgil,[13] a devotion that extended to the physical remains of the poet when Silius bought and restored Virgil's tomb; Silius also religiously celebrated the birthday of Virgil. In Hannibal's oath at the shrine of Dido, which is also the poem's promise to remain faithful to the *Aeneid* in

---

[9] Hannibal may be thought of as the 'thunderbolt' of Juno, the one that she had wished for at *Aen.* 1.39–45; Barkas, the cognomen of Hannibal's father Hamilcar, means 'thunderbolt'; cf. *Pun.* 15.664 'Hannibal the unpredictable thunderbolt of Carthage'.   [10] As Virgil's Dido had herself predicted: see p. 41 above.

[11] With *Pun.* 1.114–15, cf. *Aen.* 4.384–6.

[12] For this kind of taking up of a Virgilian 'challenge', cf. Columella 10 (on gardening) taking the *praeteritio* of *Geo.* 4.116 ff. at face value.   [13] *Ep.* 3.7.

exchange for the release of the model's creative powers, we may also read the man Silius' cultivation of the shade of Virgil in the hope of his own poetic birth (or rebirth).

Epic both before and after Virgil had its influential detractors in antiquity. Callimachus' strictures on the Telchines have largely determined the modern attitude to the lost epics of the Hellenistic world; Juvenal in his first satire, ultimately repeating the Callimachean move, contemptuously rejects the mythological epics unthinkingly churned out (according to him) in the recitation halls, and chooses the more 'relevant' and less hackneyed path of satire on contemporary *mores*. The passage is characteristic both of Juvenal's unfairness (he omits any mention of historical epic on Roman themes) and of his sharpness: his list of epic commonplaces includes the grove of Mars, Aeolus' cave of the winds, the epic storm, tortures of the damned in the Underworld, the 'theft' of the Golden Fleece, and the battle of the Centaurs. The first four of these are, literally or figuratively, places of Hellish energy; behind the sneer Juvenal captures something essential in the Flavian epic. He is deliberately blind to the possibility that the exotic themes of mythological epic might be read as figuratively relevant to the present day; after Virgil could any mythological epic escape such a reading? Juvenal represents his own poetic impulse as an irresistible *indignatio*, 'indignant anger', aroused by the contemplation of present-day Rome; even in the act of rebelling against the pressure to listen to, if not to write, epic he exploits an emotion related to the Hellish anger that motivates much epic.

Men, beasts and gods: Herculean efforts

If the full-blown introduction of a dualistic world-picture into the epic seems to be a Virgilian innovation, determinative for the course of epic over the better part of two millennia, it is not a creation *ex nihilo*. To begin with it can be regarded as a transformation of the basic epic (Homeric and Hesiodic) division between men and gods, earth and Olympus. Much recent criticism, both structuralist and more traditional, has identified as a central focus of interest of archaic Greek *epos* the definition of the limits and aspirations of men by reference to the similarities and dissimilarities between the 'godlike hero' and the true gods. Structuralist analysis sets this opposition of man and god within a three-term series of beast, man and god:[14] man attempts to establish a

---

[14] Classically in Vernant (1981), Detienne (1981). See also Rieks (1967).

firm footing on his isthmus of humanity between the dangerous seas of bestiality and godhead. One of the services of structuralist analysis has been to reveal the impossibility of finally separating the beast and the god: in the realm of the non-human, distinctions tend to collapse. Beast–man–god is a series that readily translates into the series Hell – earth – Heaven: through surrender to the passions and violence that he shares with the beasts man bestializes himself and may condemn himself to endless torments in a Hell peopled with nightmare versions of the wild animals of this world (in the *Aeneid* the cries of the damned in Tartarus and those of Circe's beasts sound the same, 6.557 and 7.15); while through cultivation of the divine spark man may attain the self-control and happiness of the gods in this life, and in the next become an inhabitant of Heaven or of the very similar neighbourhood of the Elysian Fields.

It is an irony that there is no surviving ancient epic on Hercules, and yet he is in many ways the epic hero *par excellence*, the epic hero as fully realized in his tendency to excess, whose exploits are already a ghostly presence in the Odyssean *Nekyia*. Hercules is the hero who most starkly in one person incorporates the alternatives of man, beast or god. Like Achilles he is a congenitally unstable character because of his dual parentage, divine on one side and human on the other, but unlike Achilles he ultimately succeeds in converting his godlikeness into godhead, but not before he has experienced bestiality in several figurative forms. He is also the hero who most completely explores the spatial limits of the Virgilian and post-Virgilian epic journey, plumbing the depths of Hell and finishing his career with the ascent to Heaven. Hercules figures in a nodal episode of the *Aeneid*, and on other occasions is the explicit or implicit model for the exploits of other heroes (programmatically for the 'labours' (*Aen.* 1.10) of Aeneas). Significantly those critics intent on dissolving Virgil's 'Augustanism' have a field-day with the Hercules and Cacus episode in *Aeneid* 8, superficially one of the most schematically dualistic of the poem, but where it is notoriously hard to distinguish between the emotions and tactics of the 'evil' Cacus and the champion of 'good man' Evander.[15] None of the imperial Latin epics tells the story of Hercules directly, but it might be fair to label the post-Virgilian series as, in important respects, 'Herculean epic'. In the *Metamorphoses* Hercules appears only as one character among many; but in Lucan the Hercules

---

[15] See pp. 22–3 above; Feeney (1991) 158–9.

and Antaeus episode in book 4 has functions analogous to those of Virgil's Hercules and Cacus, and Caesar and Cato represent active and contemplative versions of the Herculean hero. Hercules is a central actor in Valerius' *Argonautica* until his premature separation from the expedition, after which he is an absent standard for the heroics of the others, as in the Apollonian model.[16] In Silius Hercules is almost monotonously present as a model for the great men of both Rome and Carthage, above all Scipio and Hannibal.[17] The ease with which the greatest pagan hero becomes a *Hercules Christianus* allows for a smooth transition from imperial to Christian epic.

At the heart of Anchises' revelation of the future history of Rome in *Aeneid* 6 is a comparison of Augustus and Hercules. In book 8 Evander defends the worship of Hercules (the only foreign worship countenanced by Romulus) as not being the product of vain superstition or a slight on the old gods. It is a little odd for the *Greek* Evander to make a defence appropriate to a Roman, and his defensiveness conceals the more important point that it is the Roman *princeps* who innovates by putting Hercules at the centre of Rome, in the person of *himself*. Hercules becomes the imperial hero above all. But official imperial imagery scarcely contains and controls the figure of Hercules: like Hercules the emperor may turn out to be saviour or savage; imperial Rome may be a version of Heaven or of Hell. The godlike, even divine, emperor may all too quickly turn into a raging beast indiscriminate in his anger – *the* epic emotion, and the one that was most dangerous for a subject in the *princeps*.[18] The epic journey is typically one from Hell to Heaven; in historical reality (or rather in the Roman historians' version of reality) the recurrent sequence is the reverse: an emperor who starts off well, living up to the inaugural imagery of the Golden Age returned, but who at some point goes bad. The outstanding example of this biographical tradition is Nero, a ruler who starts off as an obedient practitioner of good kingship guided by the philosopher Seneca, but who ends up as a tyrant more cruel and arbitrary than anything that the wicked East could provide. Lucan's epic was written during the later years of Nero's reign; the surviving Flavian epics were all begun within twenty years of the civil

---

[16] See pp. 36 above.   [17] Bassett (1966).

[18] Virgil explores the anger of civil war; Ovid first feels and writes about the anger of the emperor. Horace, *Ep.* 1.2.13–14, in the course of a moralizing summary of the Homeric poems, comments on the adverse effects of royal anger on their subjects in the *Iliad*.

war that erupted on the death of Nero. There is no obligation to believe that the angry tyrants of Statius and Silius are intended as critical of Domitian, but after the official *damnatio memoriae* the polarity of god and beast is instantly exploited by Pliny in the *Panegyricus*, praising Trajan for refusing the divine honours demanded by Domitian, and for presenting a humane face at his audiences (*Pan.* 48.3): 'we linger as if we too belonged in the house that so recently that monstrous beast had fortified with terror, like some animal shut up in a cave who now licked the blood of his relatives, now emerged for the murder and slaughter of the leading citizens'. Domitian is a savage god who demands blood: 'the terrible statues of this most cruel of masters were worshipped with as much blood of victims as the rivers of human blood that he poured out' (*Pan.* 52.7); in this last rhetorical conceit blood for the gods is equated with the blood shed by the 'beast', in the confusion of a 'sacrificial crisis'.[19]

Feeney traces the centrality of the beast–man–god series in Apollonius, Virgil, Ovid and Statius.[20] One might add that structures based on this series are deeply rooted in Attic tragedy,[21] and the prevalence of similar features in post-Virgilian epic may be another sign of Virgil's radical contamination of epic with tragedy. Ovid's choice of subject-matter allows him to explore the issues through the literal transformation of men into animals and gods. The first metamorphosis of an individual is of Lycaon, whose crime is to use murder to test the distinction between man and god, and who is turned by Jupiter into a wolf, a particularly ambivalent form of beast, especially for the Romans. The last metamorphoses are of Julius Caesar into a god and of Ovid into an abstract form of celestial divinity.

Lucan's Caesar, as we have seen, has features of both god and beast, possessed by the energy of both thunderbolt and lion, carving his way to the 'Heaven' of imperial apotheosis with the instruments of Hell. The *Bellum Ciuile* is not an epic of individual *aristeiai*; the one exception is the heroic defence of a Caesarian position in book 6 by the centurion Scaeva, that surrogate for his absent master, embodying the same range of

---

[19] Machiavelli says the prince must know how to use both the man and the beast; this is the significance of the legend that Achilles was educated by the centaur Chiron: 'The parable of this semi-animal, semi-human teacher is meant to indicate that a prince must know how to use both natures' (*Prince* ch. 18). Bestiality and humanity are explored at length in Statius' version of the legend in the fragmentary *Achilleid*.

[20] Feeney (1991), 94–8, 155–62, 194–8, 360–1.   [21] See e.g. Segal (1986), 26–31.

features of beast, man and god. The *aristeia* is above all a display of *uirtus*, literally 'manhood';[22] as reward for his superhuman feats Scaeva's companions worship his disfigured form as if there was a *numen* enclosed in his breast; his mortal *uirtus* is elevated to the divine status of the goddess *Virtus* (253–4). But his courage is fuelled by anger (155), and his human features are first distorted by his rage and then converted into a shapeless pulp by the wounds he receives. The narrator's similes provide an alternative commentary to the adulatory idolization of his companions (two different kinds of image-making): he is like a leopard, an African elephant, a Pannonian bear.

The death of Tydeus in Statius' *Thebaid* 8.716–66 is a very clear example of the choices available.[23] Tydeus is one of a number of Statian heroes, including Menoeceus and Capaneus, with immortal yearnings: men who feel disgust and impatience with the fragility of their mortal vessel. As he struggles with death, Minerva, the goddess of divine reason, descends to reward his virtue with immortality, but she flees in disgust as 'mindless with joy and anger' (751–2) he turns cannibal and gnaws at the head of his slayer Melanippus. In a simile (the use of the figure again alerts us to the manipulation of 'images' in a search for identity) Capaneus bringing the body of Melanippus to Tydeus is compared to Hercules bringing the Erymanthian boar to Argos. When Tydeus sets eyes on Melanippus' gasping features 'he recognised himself in him' *seseque adgnouit in illo* (753): he saw his own handiwork in the dying man; he also saw a man dying like himself (despite Minerva's plan to have it otherwise); but in this man compared to a defeated boar he also recognizes his own bestial nature. Tydeus is the boar promised by Apollo to Adrastus as a son-in-law (1.397), the man who arrives wearing on his shoulders the hide of the Calydonian boar (1.488–90). The fight within Tydeus between beast and god becomes a contest between Hell and Heaven: Tisiphone and Minerva contend for the soul of Tydeus (8.759).[24]

In book 6 of Silius' *Punica* there is a pause after the disaster of Trasimene and before the events leading to the catastrophe at Cannae, during which we are told the story of a hero of the First Punic War, Regulus.[25] The fictional audience is Regulus' own son Serranus, for whom his father's exploits function as an *exemplum* of heroism; but in

---

[22] Forms of *uirtus* or *uir* occur at 6.153, 169, 192, 240, 254, 262.
[23] Lucan's Scaeva is an important model: see esp. *Theb.* 8.700–12. On the death of Tydeus, see also p. 37 above; Feeney (1991), 360–1.   [24] See Rieks (1967), 216.
[25] *Punica* 6 makes significant use of both Lucan's Scaeva and Statius' Tydeus.

Regulus we are also introduced to a revaluation of the nature of epic heroism that will be continued in the figures of Fabius Cunctator and Scipio Africanus. Regulus displays 'the better fortitude Of patience and heroic martyrdom',[26] and in so doing seems to his son to become more than human (416–17): 'great father, than whom no greater divinity sits on the Tarpeian rock'. Serranus remembers the time when, as a small child, he saw his father return to Rome as a prisoner of the Carthaginians (426): 'his appearance was greater than human'.[27] It is gently done: a son's adulation and the exaggerated memories of childhood intimate a divinity that also derives from the literary model of Lucan's Cato, the perfect Stoic 'divine man'.[28] Regulus soars high above the bestial in man; rather the 'bestial anger' of his Carthaginian torturers (6.531) is powerless against his *uirtus*. This final resistance of Regulus to bestial enemies echoes the first exploit of his that Marus relates to Serranus, the killing of a monstrous and Hellish dragon on the shores of the African river Bagrada. This episode has a number of models, including the fight between Hercules and Cacus in *Aeneid* 8, and like the Virgilian episode is polysemous. At one level we can take the story as a prefiguration of the ultimate Roman defeat of Hannibal who is elsewhere shown under the image of a serpent; but it may also be read as psychomachy, Regulus' conquest of the serpentine passions in the human breast.[29] Marus has just introduced his narrative by calling his former master 'that sacred man, inferior to no divinity' (6.123–4).[30] There is a complication, however. It turns out that this hideous beast was a servant of the river nymphs, and retribution follows. Regulus' dashing military career is cut off when he is captured through a trick by Xanthippus. Regulus up to this point is the typical hero of the epic battlefield, whose reason may be less adequate than his spirit and courage. Is this the point of the curious detail which flaws the defeat of the dragon, that Regulus' conquest of the animal

---

[26] *Paradise Lost* 9.31–2.

[27] The language suggests the sacralization of the Roman general who devotes himself to the powers below to ensure victory for his side (Livy 8.9.10, Stat. *Theb.* 10.757).

[28] In fact Regulus has features of both Cato and Pompey in Lucan.

[29] In the background may also be sensed the godlike Cato's march through the monstrous serpents of the Libyan desert in Lucan *Bell. Ciu.* 9.

[30] *sacer ille et numine nullo|inferior*, forming a ring with 416–17 *quo maius numine nobis|Tarpeia nec in arce sedet*. At 131–2 Marus says that the goddess *Fides* had taken up residence in Regulus' breast, much as Scaeva's companions see *Virtus* lodged in his perforated breast.

within him is as yet imperfect?[31] To kill the dragon Regulus needs the helping hand of his faithful Marus and the rest of the army; only later is he perfected as the *unus homo*, as he is accompanied to the torture chamber by Marus, now the helpless spectator of a single man's heroic and victorious endurance. Regulus is enclosed in an 'iron maiden', but he is proof because *Fides* herself resides within his breast (6.130–1).[32]

Dualisms tragic and didactic

Other literary precedents condition the Virgilian version of an epic Heaven and Hell. One influence may have been the exegetical tradition: commentaries tend to schematize, especially those of an allegorical bent whose aim is to reveal conceptual or philosophical structures supporting the weave of a text. Modern readers may find it hard to make moral distinctions between the two sides in the Iliadic theomachy, but some ancient commentators saw in Athene's support of the Greeks a symbol of the divine aid that is rightfully afforded to those who fight with justice and wisdom on their side.

Virgil very deliberately created an epic that displayed the universality of the genre by incorporating elements from the whole range of ancient literary genres, but the single most important type of model other than the epic is tragedy. It is in tragedy that we find, occasionally, the only real precedent for the dualism of the *Aeneid*. The starkest surviving example is the division between the upper and lower gods that Apollo describes in his own account of the utter hatefulness of the Erinyes in the *Eumenides*.[33] The importance of the tragic model extends further, for tragedy was the genre which in fifth-century Athens had most profoundly

---

[31] Another model for the killing of a sacred dragon is Cadmus and the dragon of Mars in Ovid *Met.* 3, where the dragon is literally incorporated in human beings through the descent of the Thebans from the 'Sown Men' who sprang from its teeth. Pentheus' destructive rage is the rage of the serpent. The whole of Ovid's Theban episode is an indirect reflection on the place of anger and bestiality in Rome itself: Hardie (1990a). There are also echoes of the Fabii episode in *Fasti* 2: see Harries (1991), 156–7.

[32] The torture device is perhaps like a beast: cf. the Bull of Phalaris. Regulus is immune to the bestialization that, according to Seneca, *De ira* 3.17.2–4, affects victim as well as torturer.

[33] Hardie (1991a). Ahl (1986), 2890 ff. for parallels between the Altar of Clemency in Stat. *Theb.* 12 and the Areopagus in Aesch. *Eum.*; Statius reworks the Virgilian use of Aeschylus at the end of the *Aeneid*.

exploited the traditional myths in order to articulate the social and political problems of the city; by putting tragic dilemmas and concepts at the centre of his epic (and departing from earlier and simpler panegyrical or commemorative models of epic narrative) Virgil created the conditions for an imperial epic, whether historical or legendary, that continued to engage with the problems of the principate. The mythological tragedies of Seneca speak directly to the problems of the contemporary exercise of imperial power; this is one reason why Seneca found the cosmic and dualist patterns in Virgil so congenial.

A less expected, but determinative, influence on Virgil comes from hexameter didactic. Hesiod is already important as the source of much of the Gigantomachic material in Virgil, and his genealogical tabulation of the gods who divide the universe between them has a strong tendency to a dualism of light and dark (a source for Aeschylean theology). But paradoxically it is Lucretius, the Epicurean demolisher of the religious world-view, who vividly and powerfully revalues and then reinstates a religious dualism in his *De rerum natura*. The Epicurean poet divides the mental universe into a pre-philosophical Hell (at the end of book 3 we are presented with an elaborate allegorization of the traditional physical tortures in the Underworld in terms of the self-inflicted mental sufferings of the unenlightened), set against the undisturbed Paradise of the wise man (the Homeric picture of the ever serene mountain Olympus provides an allegory of spiritual well-being at the beginning of book 3). Lucretius is unshakeable in his certainties: the passage from the darkness of pre-philosophical misery to Epicurean illumination admits of no doubt or turning back. For Lucretius all is clear-cut, but there are two ways in which his use of Heaven and Hell might be used in more anxious ways in a non-philosophical poem: firstly his use of this-worldly allegorizations of the Underworld and of the abode of the gods leads to many versions of the confusion of the tripartite division of the universe into Hell, Earth and Heaven, in authors not blessed with the Epicurean certitude that Hell and Heaven are *not* sources of theological power. Secondly, Lucretius' epic of knowledge raises the question of the ability of the human mind to distinguish clearly between good and evil. For the complete Epicurean all is crystal clear, but delusion is the condition of the unenlightened man. Heaven and Hell are really the same thing, this physical world, but viewed through different sets of spectacles. In mythological terms Venus may be both the beneficent spirit of fertile generation or the maleficent witch of sterile erotic obsession. Virgil's use of Lucretius imparts to the

Roman epic tradition a strong philosophical streak, which foregrounds the difficulty of achieving a correct assessment of the true values of things.[34]

The confusion of Heaven and Hell in Virgil

In fact at the end of the *Aeneid* there is some considerable doubt that we have in fact travelled from Hell to Heaven; many (perhaps most) critics have felt that Aeneas' killing of Turnus leaves us at best in a murky in-between state, if not with a political and psychological failure. In terms of the theological and topographical distinction between Heaven and Hell the problem is concentrated in the very surprising way that Jupiter, for his last intervention in human affairs, employs not Mercury but a *Dira*, a Fury, to frighten off Turnus' sister Juturna. We are told that this is not an extraordinary measure for an extraordinary situation, but that two *Dirae* sit perpetually at the throne of Jupiter. Our faith in the geography of the universe that had been built up during the poem, with a serene and reasonable Jupiter enthroned in the aether, poles apart from the depths of Tartarus whence Juno summons the embodiment of evil, Allecto, for her purposes, is shattered. *Dei ira*, the just anger of Jupiter, turns out to be a *Dira*, a Fury.[35] Aeneas' final outburst of fury and anger is indistinguishable (as a psychological state) not only from the frenzy that sent him into battle in Troy but also from the devilishly inspired fury that impelled Turnus to war in book 7. In chapter 2 I analysed the problem of making distinctions between the two sides with the help of Girard's concept of the 'sacrificial crisis'. Here I approach the same phenomena from the point of view of the symbolic geography of the Virgilian universe.

In fact we do not have to wait until the end of the poem to suspect that Earth and Hell, and even Heaven and Hell, cannot be kept apart: in book 2 when the truth is finally revealed to Aeneas by his mother he sees that the Hell on Earth that is the Sack of Troy is the result of the activity of the Olympian gods;[36] in book 3 Aeneas confronts monsters with Hellish or

---

[34] Perhaps reinforced by a dose of scepticism: see Murrin (1980), ch. 2.

[35] For the ancient derivation of *Dira* from *dei ira*, see Maltby (1991), *dirus*.

[36] The sacked city as Hell reappears in Statius' description of the panic at Thebes, at *Theb.* 10.556–9, a sight that would shock even Mars, that connoisseur of things Hellish; and in an extended version in Silius' account of the destruction of Saguntum, also in book 2 of his epic (see pp. 81–3 below).

chthonic associations in the Harpies, Charybdis, Etna and Polyphemus; in book 4 Dido binds herself to the Underworld through magic ritual before making the final descent; books 5 and 6 present more benign accounts of the link between upper and lower worlds in the funeral games for Anchises and in Aeneas' *katabasis*. In book 7 the eschatological landscapes of 6 are projected on to earth, and the eternal arrangements of the afterlife recur alarmingly in a temporal succession in Aeneas' first experience of Italy, the promised land that quickly turns into an Inferno of something like civil war; in book 8 the fight between Hercules and Cacus provides a model for a (superficially) satisfactory resolution of the struggle between Heaven and Hell. In book 9 Nisus and Euryalus wander through their own infernal landscape of nocturnal slaughter and dark woods before meeting their literal deaths.[37] Perhaps Jupiter's use of the Fury should not come as such a surprise.

The endless debate among critics as to whether Virgil means us to approve or disapprove of the actions of Aeneas and his avatar Augustus is usually conducted on the level of morality or character, often by an appeal to the modern critic's construction of an ideal of humanity. But it is possible to transpose it to other levels, mythological, theological or epistemological. In the myths on which many epics are based the question of moral justification is often secondary compared with the demonstration of superior power, whether physical or intellectual. Fontenrose concludes his study of ancient myths of dragon- and giant-slaying, *Python*, with these words: 'it becomes apparent that both creative and destructive forces are mingled on both sides of the divine combat. So myth is nearer to reality in this respect than that sort of partisanship in life or that sort of melodrama in literature which pits pure good on one side against pure evil on the other.'[38] Now it is precisely the tendency of the *Aeneid* to install in the epic a partisanship that pits evil against good, yet at the same time radically to problematize that opposition. Good may be perverted into an evil parody of itself; or it may simply be intellectually difficult to distinguish between good and bad. Lucretius broods over Virgil: for the confident Epicurean the beliefs of the non-Epicurean may bear strange analogies to the truth, but once the 'parody' is seen for what it is there is no further danger of idolatry. Virgil is fascinated by this view of the world, but incapable of the Lucretian

---

[37] See Putnam (1965), 48–63.   [38] Fontenrose (1959), 473.

certitude; whence a dualism that is not finally able to keep apart order and disorder, Heaven and Hell.

The uncertainty of the *Aeneid* is the source of an important strand of continuity in post-Virgilian epic, a kind of imitation that is at the same time criticism and correction of the model, the *Aeneid*, but insofar as it represents a divergence from the *Aeneid* it is a divergence that is already present as a (de-)structuring feature within the model. There are also analogies with central aspects of the epic of Spenser and Milton, where the basic Christian dualism between the sun of righteousness and the prince of darkness is often developed in terms of a demonic parody or copy of the divine original (Satan as God's ape); Northrop Frye, in an essay on the imagery of *The Faerie Queene*, uses the term 'symbolic parody'.[39] John Steadman also discusses the parodic quality of diabolic imitation: 'Another method of presenting the conflict of Truth and Error was to embody true and false values in similar but antithetical figures.'[40] In the case of Milton this has led to an enduring critical dispute as to whether the parody may not be more truly admirable or valuable than the original. There is a parallel between the debate whether Milton was, or should have been, of the devil's party, and the central critical issue of much of twentieth-century Virgilian criticism: was Virgil for or against Aeneas and his antitype Augustus? The two debates seem to have developed independently of each other. With Milton the contrasting claims of God and Satan for the admiration of the reader arise out of the thematization within the epic narrative of the need to make a choice, intellectual and moral, between good and evil, such being the condition of our fallen selves once the apple has been tasted. It is also a condition of the fallen state that the choice is made more difficult by the frequent close resemblance of good and evil. Dante, Spenser and Milton all write a *Christian* 'epic of knowledge'. But it is at least worth asking whether there is a precedent in pagan epic. Choices, of the sort that will later become tragic, are central to the plot of the *Iliad*, though not of the *Odyssey*; Virgil added something new to the tradition when he drew the philosophical poem of Lucretius to the centre of his version of the Homeric epic; Lucretius' insistence on the distinction between the false goods of the unenlightened person immersed in the affairs of the world

---

[39] Frye (1963).
[40] Steadman (1967), 53–6, 81. Cf. also Greenblatt (1980), 76, 81–2 on the 'demonic Other'.

and the true goods of the philosopher withdrawn into himself, has at least something to do with the *Aeneid's* perpetual worrying away at the question of how to choose between public and private fulfilments, a choice that every critic of Virgil seems impelled to make anew. The most philosophically minded of Virgil's successors, Lucan, returns on several occasions to the question of knowledge, and in particular of forbidden knowledge, in the contexts of access to the prophetic secrets of Heaven and Hell and to the secrets of nature; Caesar's obsession in book 10 with the sources of the Nile symbolizes man's possibly impious curiosity about ultimate origins. Statius likewise moralizes on the unhealthiness of man's desire to know the future.

In conclusion, the *Aeneid* is an epic that strives for an unusual degree of closure, and which employs unusually schematic conceptual and cosmographic structures to this end, but at the same time is unusually prone to doubt and irresolution. It is a Virgilian realization of the tension at the heart of the genre: epic is a form that aims at definitiveness and comprehensiveness and is yet made for continuation and second thoughts. Stability but also mutability, in itself an unstable compound. Because the great national epic is not a perfectly enclosed whole, it challenges rewritings of itself. The unresolved tensions in the model hold an energy that is tapped by subsequent epicists, who may adjust the balance in favour of either Heaven or Hell, but who, insofar as they are faithful to the Virgilian project, hand over in turn a tradition that contains the seeds of further powerful reworkings. To adapt the Lucretian allegory, each new imperial epic poet is a Sisyphus who once again takes on the impossible task of rolling the stone to the top of the hill.

The confusion of Earth and Hell, and of Heaven and Hell in post-Virgilian epic

Virgil gives us two versions of the Underworld in *Aeneid* 6 and 7, the first a map of divine order and providence, suitable setting for Rome's glorious history, the second a source of uncontrolled negative energy. Through various devices of repetition between the two books Virgil suggests that it may not in fact be easy to keep the two separate. Lucan picks up the hint, and violently merges the two episodes into one in the *nekyia* of book 6 of his own epic, in the narrative of Erictho and the corpse.[41] The ways in which this mirrors *Aeneid* 6 have been exhaustively analysed: Erictho plays the role of the Sibyl who guides Aeneas through the Underworld. But it is not just a question of creating an 'anti-Sibyl' on the basis of the one Virgilian model: Erictho is also a version of Allecto in *Aeneid* 7. At the beginning of the necromancy she puts on 'the dress of a Fury' and binds her hair with vipers (*Bell. Ciu* 6.654–6); later she lashes the reluctant corpse with a living snake (727), the gesture of Allecto in her anger with Turnus (*Aen.* 7.451; possibly the lashing is inflicted with the snakes of the previous line). Erictho's invocation of the greatest powers of Hell opens with the names of Tisiphone and Megaera, omitting the name of the third sister, Allecto – perhaps because that would be in a sense to invoke herself. Finally her double assault on the reluctant corpse is like Allecto's twofold approach to Turnus (*Aen.* 7.415–66). The corpse tells of an inversion of the customary state of things in the Underworld, with the previous inhabitants of Elysium in profound sorrow and the criminals of Tartarus rejoicing (6.779–99). The place where Erictho performs necromancy can be securely located neither in the world above nor the world below (6.651–3).

Liminality and marginality are recurrent themes in Statius.[42] The liminal figure of the *Thebaid* is Oedipus, and we have already seen how his life-in-death embodies the theme of Hell on Earth; he returns to close the main action at 11.580–2 'when the father heard that crime had run its full course he burst out of the deep shadows, and displayed death unfinished at the cruel threshold'

> at genitor sceleris comperto fine profundis
> erupit tenebris, saeuoque in limine profert
> mortem imperfectam.

[41] This *contaminatio* is the reverse of the *dédoublement* whereby features of *Aeneid* 6 are spread over both books 5 and 6 of the *Bellum Ciuile*. But the doubling involved in the episodes of Appius at Delphi and Sextus and Erictho is also an imitation of the doubling of Underworld episodes in the central books, 6 and 7, of the *Aeneid*. In *Bell. Ciu.* 5 there is a confusion of above and below in the suggestion that Apollo, the god of light, has buried himself at Delphi as a chthonic god of prophecy (5.82–5).

[42] Ahl (1986), 2898–903 is eloquent on the confusion of boundaries and definitions in the *Thebaid* as the result of a perverted logic built into the pursuit of power. This he sees as 'the tale of man himself'; my analysis is intended to show how these confusions may be understood as a *generic* property of epic, that speaks closely to a particularly Roman experience of history. Statian dualism (and its confusion) is also discussed by Feeney (1991), 344–64.

The ambiguities proliferate: the living Oedipus returns to the world of light at the end of the story (*fine*), but he brings with him a state of half-life and half-death (*mortem imperfectam*). Fittingly he halts at the threshold, and *saeuo* suggests that this is no mortal threshold, but the door to Hell itself. The position of *sceleris* teases: does it go with what follows ('hearing of the end of the crime'), or with what precedes (Oedipus is 'the begetter of crime')? His movement into the world above crosses the descent of his sons into Tartarus (11.574–5), but how great really is the distance between Hell and the Hell on Earth that we have just witnessed? The poet's prayer to the goddesses of the Styx to spare man henceforth is met by the emergence of a semi-human form compared in a simile to Charon (587–92). Oedipus' life-in-death is repeated and avenged in the very manner of Polynices' death: the mortally wounded Eteocles pretends to be dead, but the 'dead' man has just enough life left to kill his duped brother (11.554–5 'already in the middle of death he plots his last trick' *fraudemque supremam|in media iam morte parat*). Polynices' dying words hint at the true nature of this survival after death (568): 'do you live or is it your anger that still survives?' *uiuisne an adhuc manet ira superstes . . ?* At 564 Polynices had been in the position of Aeneas at the end of the *Aeneid*, 'standing over his defeated enemy' (*superstantem*), but it turns out that it is really anger that 'stands over' or 'survives' (*superstes*). Anger survives the tomb; there is always anger left over for the next battle (or for the next epic).[43] The more men anger kills, the greater is the power of this Hellish Fury in the human breast.

In some ways the presiding god of the *Thebaid* is the god of war, Mars; at times he verges on being little more than a personification of the spirit of battle-anger but insofar as he maintains his full personality as one of the Olympians there is an ambivalence as to whether he properly belongs in the upper or lower worlds. This ambivalence is worked skilfully through the detailed combinatorial imitation of Virgilian models that typifies all of the epicists under discussion: for example at the beginning of book 7 of the *Thebaid* Jupiter, the supreme Olympian, sends Mercury down to earth to rouse Mars to inspire Argos with war-fever against Thebes.[44] Structurally this corresponds to Juno's intervention in book 7

---

[43] Cf. the seer Mopsus' account of the refusal of those killed by deliberate violence to lie down at Val. Flacc. *Argon.* 3.384–90, beginning 'anger remains and the pain endures' *ira manet duratque dolor*, with verbal echoes of *Aen.* 1.25–6 telling of the ineradicable causes of the anger of Juno that motivates the *Aeneid*.

[44] Mercury's storm-tossed voyage may have been one of the models for Milton's journey of Satan through Chaos.

of the *Aeneid*, using a creature of Hell, Allecto, to inflame the Italians against the Trojans; the structural correspondence in itself, once recognized, arouses unease at what Jupiter is doing here.[45] But the immediate Virgilian model for the despatch of Mercury is the passage in book 4 of the *Aeneid* where Jupiter sends his messenger to rouse Aeneas into leaving Dido and Carthage; in a traditional epic equipping-scene, Virgil describes the various attributes that Mercury dons for his journey, including the wand with which he guides souls to and from the Underworld. Mercury (Hermes) is, as the messenger of Jupiter, he who has the power to cross the boundary between upper and lower worlds; but in Virgil's Dido-story these details are not the result merely of the inertia of the formulaic epic tradition, for the final consequence of Mercury's mission will be Dido's passage to the Underworld as she dies by her own hand (and the point is reinforced by the final lines of the book which tell of Juno sending down her messenger, Iris, to ease Dido from her death agony into the next world). Statius reworks the Virgilian allusion to the infernal aspect of Mercury into a more immediate version of the Underworld, for the 'House' of Mars (7.40–63) is described through a patchwork of references to Virgilian descriptions of the Underworld, particularly from book 6 of the *Aeneid*. Does Jupiter communicate with his son, one of the Olympians, or with a brother of the Furies?

War, the traditional epic theme, produces a Hell on Earth. When the physical division between Earth and Hell is miraculously breached at the end of *Thebaid* 7 as the ground parts to swallow up the priest-warrior Amphiaraus, the 'infernal bellowing' (7.797) is mistaken by the combatants for the din of war. The end of the first day's fighting is marked by a cataclysmic confusion of above and below; the opening of Hell that was a figure of speech for Hercules' tearing open of Cacus' cave in *Aeneid* 8 becomes literal reality (816–17), and the object of Pluto's complaint at the beginning of book 8. He interprets this physical confusion of the

[45] Cf. the combination of models from *Aeneid* 1 and 7 in Jupiter's first speech at *Theb.* 1.214–47. That council ends with the oath by Styx, traditional but here reinforcing the ominous bond between Jupiter and the Underworld. Mercury is also here the intermediary between Heaven and Hell, sent to Pluto to summon the shade of Laius. Ahl (1986), 2844 notes a nice moment at *Theb.* 2.115–16 where the disguised ghost of Laius, adapting the words of Mercury at *Aen.* 4.268, tells Eteocles 'the father of the gods himself took pity and sent me to you *ab alto*', where *ab alto* is ambiguous between 'from on high' and 'from the depths': 'Literally the ghost comes from the underworld; but he is sent by Jupiter "on high".'

79

upper and lower worlds as a sign of strife within the family of gods, civil war between himself and his brother (8.36). His reaction is defiant (37): 'then let there be an end to the distinctions of the universe' *pereant agedum discrimina rerum*, and he orders Tisiphone to ascend and provoke fraternal strife and an assault on the gods; in his final words he compares the invasion of Hades to the Giants' attack on Heaven by piling Pelion on Ossa (79). Thus Amphiaraus' downward movement into Hades is the excuse for yet another repetition of Allecto's ascent to the upper airs in *Aeneid* 7. The final staging of Hell on Earth comes in book 11 with the climactic duel between the two brothers: the two sisters Tisiphone and Megaera range over the earth unopposed (11.57–112, 403–23, 457–96). At the last even the Furies stand aside to watch: Hell hath no Furies like – men (537–8): 'There is no longer any work for the Furies; they merely marvel as applauding spectators, and are envious that human fury is more powerful than they.'[46] The psychological and social reality underlying the cosmological and theological images of evil is laid bare.

The priestly mantle of the unwitting offender Amphiaraus is taken up by Thiodamas; his first act on his inauguration is to sing a hymn to Earth in which he attempts to affirm the cosmic distinctions just now effaced (8.303–38). This is the map of the universe from which the post-Virgilian epic takes the co-ordinates of its heroic and divine action, and which it so consistently seeks to throw into confusion. In this *physikos hymnos* the echoes of Lucretius are manifest; it was the Lucretian vision of an ordered universe that Virgil wished to share, but could not.[47]

In Silius the moral and theological dualism of the Virgilian tradition is presented in a stark and schematic form: Roman *fides* versus Carthaginian *perfidia*, the heavenly Jupiter and his representatives against the Hellish Juno and Hannibal; Hannibal attempts to be another Hercules but succeeds only in playing the role of a Titan or Giant.[48] It is true that along the way Silius plays with ambivalence, and where he does he is often indebted to Lucan: Hannibal *does* have some claim to our admiration as a Herculean and demonic hero. There is more than a hint of Lucan's Caesar in him, and he is a fairly close relative also of Milton's Satan. Rome is not always true to an ideal of rational virtue; even in that

[46] See p. 44 above.

[47] At the end of the *Thebaid* Theseus fights for those same 'terrestrial and universal laws' *terrarum leges et mundi foedera* (12.642) that Thiodamas had hymned in vain.

[48] On the opposition of 'Herculean' and 'Titanic' paths to the sky, see Dauge (1981).

time of national emergency Silius shows us the presence of the divisive forces that were to explode in the war between Pompey and Caesar.[49] But finally there is no real doubt about the victory of light over dark.

Silius rings the changes on the motif of war as Hell on Earth. Among the omens that presage disaster at Lake Trasimene the lake itself exhales a black fog like an Avernus (5.34–7); the trap into which the Romans fall is easy to enter, but there is no way back – 'easy is the descent to Avernus'.[50] In book 7 a rash engagement of Hannibal by Minucius is framed by Hellish allusion: at 585–6 in his moment of despair Minucius 'had mentally already crossed the Styx to the place of eternal darkness'; when Fabius has charged in to repel Hannibal, then (723–4) 'at last was dispelled the Stygian darkness in which the black storm of the Carthaginians had shrouded Minucius' forces'. Somewhat surprisingly little use is made of the motif in the enormously long narrative of the battle of Cannae, but one may note the way in which the battle spreads to the gods (9.288–9): 'the madness of strife entered the sky and forced the gods to war'. *Discordia demens* is the Fury-like personification that sits at the threshold of the Virgilian Underworld (*Aen.* 6.280; *Bellum* is in the line before). The confusion of Heaven and Hell is thus presented in the extreme form of the invasion of Heaven by a spirit of Hell; the consequence is that Heaven is deserted as the gods descend to Earth to do battle (9.303).

These are incidental allusions: a large-scale drama opposing Heaven and Hell is staged in the city of Saguntum in book 2. Hannibal's attack on the Spanish town was the occasion for the outbreak of the Second Punic War; Silius devotes much of his first two books to a narrative of the siege and sack, and the episode bears a heavy symbolism (of a kind thoroughly Virgilian in technique).[51] So heavy is the symbolism that the historical city is almost lost to sight: Saguntum is another Troy, and just as the sack

[49] See Hardie (1993b).

[50] *Aen.* 6.126 *facilis descensus Auerno.* The language of *Pun.* 5.41 'an unguarded shore from which there will soon be no return' *incustoditum, mox irremeabile, litus* plays with *Aen.* 6.424–5 'Aeneas hurries to enter after burying the watch-dog in sleep and swiftly makes his way past the shore of the waters of no return' *occupat Aeneas aditum custode sepulto euaditque|celer ripam irremeabilis undae.*

[51] See Vessey (1974), who does not make enough allowance for the paradoxes and confusion in the episode. McGuire (1990), 40, sees 'the complete disorder operating at heavenly, earthly, and infernal levels' at Saguntum as a prefiguration of civil war at Rome, the final outcome of the historical processes set in motion by the defeat of Hannibal.

of Virgil's Troy is a model for the sacks of Carthage and of Alba Longa, and, by inversion, for the founding of Rome, so the sack of Saguntum is an image of what Hannibal desires, ultimately in vain, to do to Rome, and of what will eventually happen to Carthage. The earthly city also becomes the scene of a conflict between Heaven and Hell, embodied respectively in the personification of *Fides*, an inhabitant of the sky, called upon by Hercules as a primal and all-powerful divinity in another imitation of Lucretius' opening hymn to Venus (2.484–92), and the Fury Tisiphone, called up from the depths of Hell by Juno in yet another reworking of *Aeneid* 7. One may compare the confrontation between *Pietas* and Tisiphone before the duel of Polynices and Eteocles in book 11 of Statius' *Thebaid*, in which the Fury wins out. Piety *might* have prevented the Statian duel; Silius' Saguntum is in a no-win position, and the effects of *Fides* and Tisiphone are disconcertingly alike: both inspire the Saguntines with a desire for death, *Fides* through the valiant death in battle that Aeneas at first longs for in book 2 of the *Aeneid*, and Tisiphone through a glorious mass suicide. The Fury, in the disguise of Tiburna, presents suicide as an escape from the doomed city, using the words with which in *Aeneid* 2 the ghost of Hector urged Aeneas to flee from Troy and *not* to seek death in battle. The two choices open to Aeneas at Troy are at Saguntum reduced to one inevitability: death. It is even more disconcerting to find the effects of Virgil's Allecto on her human victims echoed not only in the workings of Silius' Tisiphone, but also in *Fides*' inspiration of the Saguntines (2.516–18). But if *Fides*' fine frenzy seems dubious in its excess, Juno and Tisiphone also misjudge: Juno bids Tisiphone 'send all Saguntum down to Erebus'. Her work done, the Fury returns to the lower world hurrying along the Saguntine shades with her (693–5); the narrator has other ideas, bidding the 'starry souls' to make their way to Elysium. It will be the victor Hannibal, not the vanquished, who will end up ingloriously at the Styx. Silius' manipulation of the confusions of Heaven and Hell is powerful, even if he does not avoid a residual incoherence in his effects. Much of the power derives from a reworking of Lucanian paradox: the 'perverted piety' of the scenes at 2.609–49, father killing son, husband wife, and so on, are indebted to Lucan's exploration of the paradoxes of mutual suicide when a group of Caesarian soldiers 'virtuously' commit the ultimate sin of civil war, the killing of brothers and fathers, in order to avoid capture by the enemy (*Bell. Ciu.* 4.529–81). The confusion of the effects of *Fides* and Tisiphone is also related to the ambiguities of the sacrificial suicide of Menoeceus in book 10 of Statius'

Thebaid, where a second reading will discover unsettling ambiguities in the schematic opposition of a godlike Menoeceus and a Hellish Capaneus.[52]

Valerius Flaccus' *Argonautica* is a version of the archetypal Greek myth of the questing journey. The *Argo* is traditionally the first ship, and the institution of sea-faring is a pivotal event in ancient constructions of cultural history, often marking the point at which a primitive innocence slides into a moral decline. Valerius, unlike his Greek model Apollonius of Rhodes, chooses to stress this wider historical aspect of the story: the particular adventures of Jason and his men assume a much wider importance and symbolism as a nodal point in history, in much the same way that Virgil's story of Aeneas, Lucan's account of the civil war and Silius' narrative of the war against Hannibal all reach beyond their localized plots to claim a universal significance. In the famous ode on the *Argo* in Seneca's *Medea* (301–79), the idea of a sinful infringement of the natural boundary between land and sea is joined to a fantasy of voyages to the furthest parts of the world and beyond, a fantasy that has its origins in the historical romance of Alexander wondering whether to set sail over the Ocean, and which then enters the panegyrical amplification of the extent of the Roman empire. In the proem to his *Argonautica* Valerius invites a comparison between the legendary achievement of Jason and the power of the Roman emperor by praising Vespasian's opening up of the 'Caledonian Ocean' (a reference to Claudius' expedition to Britain in A.D. 43). It would be perverse to dismiss this association of the mythical and historical as no more than a flourish of flattery.

Jason's journey may be understood as a geographical inscription of the victory of the sky-god Jupiter over chthonic opponents, the Titans and Giants. As the Argo sets out to sea, the scene switches to Heaven with an interview between Jupiter and the Sun (1.498–573) that reworks the interview between Jupiter and Venus in *Aeneid* 1. In both places Jupiter sets the immediate events of the epic within the widest historical perspective. Valerius' Jupiter approves of the sea-journey because he wishes to eliminate the idleness of 'his father's reign' (1.500), that is to say the absence of toil and labour under Saturn, in the Golden Age.[53] At the end of the scene Jupiter turns to address three of his sons who are among

---

[52] For other sacrificial complexities in this episode, see Hardie (1993b).

[53] On Valerius' thematization of the transition from the Golden to the Iron Age and the problematic nature of the first ship, see Feeney (1991), 330–5.

the crew of the *Argo*, Hercules and Castor and Pollux, and exhorts them to struggle on their journey to the stars, following their father who gained control of the world after the defeat of the Titans and Giants. The scene in Heaven is immediately followed by a reworking of the Virgilian storm in *Aeneid* 1, as Boreas goes to a Tartarean place of the winds to persuade the king of the winds, Aeolus, to grant Boreas the freedom (*libertas* 1.601) to confuse sky and sea that he enjoyed before Jupiter was king. Neptune intervenes to prevent the destruction of the *Argo*.

Hell and Heaven are emblematically opposed in the first two extended descriptions of the *Argo*'s route at the beginning of book 2. Firstly the *Argo* sails past Pallene, a traditional site of the battle between the Giants and the gods, whose sky-reaching rocks are the tomb and monument of the Giants on which Jupiter still pours down his thunderbolts, a weird kind of fossilized Gigantomachy. The sun then sets, and in this first ever night at sea the sailors are afraid of the dark, until the helmsman Tiphys cheers them by reminding them of the gods' favour in protecting them from the 'Hellish' storm of book 1, and by pointing to the stars glittering in 'the unchanging sky' (2.55) which are also their guide. Tiphys will follow not those stars like Orion and Perseus that 'fall into' (2.62) the sea, but the constellation of the Serpent that never sets. 'Following' stars is both the helmsman's immediate duty and the eventual fate of the *Argo* transferred to the sky.

As they continue on their way the Argonauts pass a number of places that bear the signs of Jupiter's victory. Their first stop is Lemnos, holy to Vulcan because it was there that he fell to earth, when Jupiter hurled him from Heaven because he tried to release Juno from chains after the other gods had attempted to rebel against Jupiter's new rule (2.82–93). On first landing they are taken by Hypsipyle to the rock that steams and smokes over the cave of Vulcan, where he makes the thunderbolt for Jupiter (2.333–9): the Underworld obedient to the will of Heaven. In book 4 the Argonauts come to the land of the Bebrycians with its murderous boxer king Amycus. This monster is repeatedly compared, explicitly and by allusion, to the Homeric and Virgilian Polyphemus, in whom some have seen a demonized version of the foreign 'other' confronted by the early Greeks on their colonizing expeditions. The boxing-match between Amycus, the son of Neptune, and Pollux, son of Jupiter, follows the model of Gigantomachy; this feature is already present in Apollonius, who does not however connect it to the wider themes as Valerius does. Neptune is already opposed to the voyage and so to Jupiter's plan.

Amycus is an outmoded and remote survival from the order of things before the rule of Jupiter, a pocket of resistance to be mopped up by the *Argo*. The last ordeal faced by the *Argo* before reaching the Black Sea is the passage of the Clashing Rocks, a manifestation of natural violence that forms a ring with the first trial, the storm in book 1. The storm winds come from deep below the earth; the simile that rounds off the episode of the Clashing Rocks compares the relief of the crew to that of Hercules and Theseus when they first re-emerged from the darkness of the Underworld (4.700–2).[54] The feeling that this voyage is closely associated with the final adjustments to the institution of Jupiter's power is reinforced by the remarkable synchronization of the arrival of the Argonauts in Colchis with the liberation by Hercules of Prometheus from his chains high on the Caucasus (5.154–76). This may also be taken as a symbol of the 'Promethean' achievement of the Argonauts in reaching a place previously barred to western man, and as such is to be taken closely with the episode that immediately precedes the passing of the Clashing Rocks, the liberation of Phineus from the Hellish Harpies, a visitation by an angry Jupiter on a human prophet who was too free with the secrets of Jupiter, a moral fable on the subject of forbidden knowledge (4.479–82).[55]

So far we have a relatively straightforward story of the extension of the power of the sky-god Jupiter at the expense of the forces of Hell;[56] a similarly comfortable schematism informs Orpheus' song of Io at 4.391–418, reworking the Virgilian opposition of a Hellish Juno and an Olympian Jupiter. But the simple scheme is easily clouded. To start with there is the matter of Jupiter and the Harpies. Already in Virgil the Harpies are identified with Furies (*Aen.* 3.214–15, 252); in Valerius they are described as 'daughters of Typhon, the wrath of the Thunderer' (4.428; cf. 474).[57] In this policing by Jupiter of the world with infernal agents we have another version of the use of a Fury by Jupiter at the end of the *Aeneid*, 12.843–68. That passage is hinted at less directly in the pair

---

[34] The story of the *Argo* may have its origins in a journey of initiation analogous to Heracles' descent to the Underworld, and Apollonius already exploits the chthonic imagery inherent in his material: see e.g. Beye (1982), 44–5, 112–14, 165–6.

[55] The association of Phineus' freedom to tell Jupiter's secrets to the Argonauts (4.559–60) with the physical passage of a perilous barrier at the end of the world invites comparison with the Lucretian motif of the intellectual adventurer's bursting out of the blazing walls that hem in the world.

[56] Note the tendency to identify Hell with an order of the past, Heaven with a present and future order.   [57] The *dei ira* etymology again (see p. 73 above).

of similes that conclude the storm scene in book I of the *Argonautica* (682–92): Jason's prayer to Neptune is compared to the vows of anxious Calabrian farmers after 'anger of the gods', *ira deum*, in the form of drought has devastated livestock and crops; next the silent obedience of the rowers to the commands of Tiphys is compared to the forces of the storm that wait for instructions by the throne of Jupiter. The net effect when we bear in mind the Virgilian *Dirae* who sit by the throne of Jupiter as instruments of his wrath (*Aen.* 12.845–52), is to suggest that although this storm was not of Jupiter's making, it is scarcely to be distinguished from those that he does unleash.

Further doubts arise when we reflect on the theme of the first ship, symbol of both man's heroic intelligence and courage and of the beginning of decline from an ideal primitive state. Neptune does indeed calm the storm that threatens the *Argo* when it first sails, but only because he relishes the prospect of all the deaths by shipwreck to come (1.647–50). This is an alternative view of the *Argo*, close to the ode in Seneca's *Medea*, that is not cancelled by the more optimistic outlook of Jupiter. The difficulty that the reader has in adjudicating between the two attitudes is akin to Virgil's deliberately ambivalent assessment of the age of Jupiter in the first *Georgic*.

If we read the first half of the *Argonautica* as a positive account of man's enforcement of a sunny, Jovian order at the expense of forces of the lower world, it is difficult to know what to make of the second half, which tells of more tyrants, bloody wars, deception and family murder. The new world seems like an even more unpleasant version of the old, repetition without significant difference. This sterile repetitiousness may itself be viewed as repetition of the Virgilian inability finally to establish the new order; Jason in his complaint to Aeetes repeats the *alius* of Virgil's Sibyl.[58] The neat map of Heaven and Hell that had been drawn by the end of *Aeneid* 6 was turned topsy-turvy when we started to read the second half of the poem in book 7, and an earthly paradise quickly turned into a Hell on Earth. The escape of the Argonauts from the Clashing Rocks, gates to the Black Sea, like an escape from Hades, invites comparison with the emergence of Aeneas from the Underworld through

[58] *Argon.* 7.92 'I see before me another Pelias, another sea of troubles' *alium hic Pelian, alia aequora cerno;* cf. *Aen.* 6.89 'another Achilles has been born in Latium' *alius Latio iam partus Achilles* (on which see p. 17 above). On arrival in Colchis the Argonauts complained that (5.298–9) 'nothing had been achieved by the discovery of the Phasis or by the taming of the waves of the Symplegades' (cf. 5.542–5).

the gate of ivory at the end of *Aeneid* 6. But on the other side Argonauts soon meet death again with the passing of Idmon and Tiphys, and versions of Allecto abound in the new land that they have come to.

If at most of their stops the voyage of the *Argo* is a benignly civilizing influence (Lemnos, Troy, Bebrycia, Phineus), on one occasion navigation, or rather its failure, is the immediate cause of mass destruction, when Tiphys falls asleep and the *Argo* drifts back to Cyzicus to be mistaken for the enemy Pelasgi. In the resulting 'Tartarean night' of slaughter (3.212) there is a veritable Hell on Earth as the Furies range freely. Gigantomachic imagery abounds, and there are hints of the Virgilian Sack of Troy. This war between allies is akin to civil war, and the inability to make the necessary discriminations almost leads to the ultimate fratricide as the twins Castor and Pollux fail to recognize each other (3.186–9). Jupiter is virtually an accessory to the fact: at 3.249 he intervenes not because he had suddenly had his attention drawn to what is going on, but because he now thinks that enough is enough. The reason for his acquiescence is presumably that the battle is ultimately the result of the anger of the Magna Mater, mother of the gods, at Cyzicus' unthinking killing of one of the lions that pulled the goddess's chariot. The invocation of Clio at the beginning of the episode concludes with two questions (3.16–18): 'Why did Jupiter allow such a battle, the clash of right hands joined in guest-friendship? Why the trumpets and the night-hag Fury's onslaught?'

> . . . cur talia passus
> arma, quid hospitiis iunctas concurrere dextras
> *Iuppiter?* unde tubae nocturnaque mouit *Erinys?*

The vocabulary and grammar record a precise distribution of active and passive responsibility between the Fury and Jupiter, but the visual effect of line 18, framed by *Iuppiter* and *Erinys*, is to suggest a tighter alliance between the two. If we are reminded of the dubious alliances at the end of the *Aeneid*, we may also reflect that in the Cyzicene episode Valerius has found a mythological episode whose pertinence to the experiences of Roman history is uncomfortably clear.

CHAPTER

4

Succession: fathers, poets, princes

Fathers and sons, husbands and wives

From its beginnings the epic's central subject may be construed as the continuity or discontinuity of social and political structures. The *Iliad* tells of a struggle to destroy the large-scale structure of the city as a means to the restoration of order within the small-scale structure of the family of Menelaus; the *Odyssey* tells of a journey towards the restoration of a family and household ruptured by the absence of the husband and father, Odysseus. In the patriarchal society of antiquity the crucial relationship for the family (and ultimately for the city) is that of father to son. Here the two Homeric epics diverge, the one having a tragic, the other a comic, plot. In the *Iliad* our attention dwells not on the future reunion of Menelaus and Helen, but on family lines extinguished: in Troy the death of Hector, sole stay of the city, before his father's eyes, entailing also the annihilation of the prospects for Hector's own son, Astyanax, the 'lord of the city' who will never grow up to fill the role for which his name marks him out. On the Greek side Achilles' decision to fulfil *his* role as 'best of the Achaeans' by returning to the battle at Troy simultaneously removes the possibility of his homecoming to a reunion with his aged father Peleus. Achilles mentions his own son Neoptolemus once only, in a speech preoccupied with grief for the dead Patroclus, who has come to represent for him all close personal relationships (*Iliad* 19.326–33). Conversely, the *Odyssey* is as much about the reunion of fathers and sons as it is about a man finding his wife. At the end of the poem Odysseus goes to find his father Laertes in the fields; earlier he has been reunited with his own son Telemachus. The first four books of the *Odyssey* are a kind of *Bildungsroman* showing the growth in Telemachus' experience and maturity as he travels in search of news of his missing father; when it comes to the killing of the suitors the son is fully adequate as his father's partner in the typically male activity of fighting. Generational continuity in this household is not, finally, in doubt.

In Rome generational continuity is stressed perhaps even more than in the Greek world. The *gens* and the gentile name are central to the upper-class Roman's sense of his identity; the ancestors are physically present in the *imagines*, the wax death-masks kept in the *atrium* of the house and worn by living members of the family in funeral processions. This literal impersonation is matched by the more general pressure to live up to, even to relive, the virtues and exploits of the ancestor with whom one shares a name. Identity is not limited to the present time or to the living body. The epic is an ideal vehicle for the representation of this conception of the relation between individual and family, because of the genre's hospitality to repetition, impersonation and possession.[1] Virgil extends a Roman antiquarian interest in family trees to an epic presentation 'in character' of ancestors of Roman *gentes*: in the ship-race in *Aeneid* 5 the Trojan Sergestus, ancestor of the *gens Sergia*, runs his ship on to the rocks with the reckless audacity with which his descendant Catiline nearly brought the Roman ship of state to disaster. Silius Italicus likewise invests some of the actors in the war against Hannibal with the characteristics of famous members of the same families from more recent history. Glancing forward to the end of the tradition, in *Paradise Lost* the motif of living up to family expectations is transposed on to a theological plane in the construction of a chain of individuals who may or may not fulfil the requirement laid on them of recognizing and faithfully imitating their progenitor (The Father – the Son/Satan – Adam – Eve – ... Milton – the reader).

There is a corresponding fear of the inability to live up to one's ancestors and of the shame attached to that inability. This is not just a Roman anxiety: in the *Iliad* Agamemnon stings Diomedes by suggesting that he is not as great a hero as his father Tydeus (*Il.* 4.365–400). But it receives more emphasis in Latin epic, where a character may be *degener*, 'degenerate', 'inferior to one's family', or act in such a way as to disprove the imputation. In *Aeneid* 2 Achilles' son Neoptolemus counters Priam's accusation that he is less merciful than his father in killing one of the Trojan king's sons with the ironic taunt that Priam should take a message

---

[1] See chapters 1 and 2.

to Achilles that his son is *degener* (*Aen.* 2.549). Imagery suggests that Neoptolemus is virtually a reincarnation of his father, fully charged with Achilles' demonic energy. A clear example of a son worse than his father is Lucan's Sextus Pompeius, 'a son unworthy of his great father', or 'a son unworthy of his father, (Pompey) the Great' (*Bell. Ciu.* 6.420 *magno proles indigna parente*). Lucan's epic is obsessed with the theme of names that have come to lack substance; here the gentile name *Pompeius* is merely a shell concealing a feeble shadow of former greatness.

The proper continuation of the male line depends on the suitably arranged union of the two sexes in marriage, whence an epic obsession with images of acceptable and (above all) unacceptable dynastic weddings. Here Virgil marks an important break with the Homeric epics, in both of which marriage is the central issue, but not with a view to the *future* procreation of heirs. Menelaus fights to regain Helen by whom he has already sired children. Odysseus labours for reunion with the wife who has already given him an heir in Telemachus. By contrast Aeneas journeys away from the wife who bore him Ascanius, Creusa, to a war for a new wife, Lavinia, who will bear him a son Silvius to rule eventually at Alba and father the dynastic line of that city. One of the two lines of descent from Aeneas thus hangs on the successful winning of the new bride.[2] The wedding of Aeneas and Lavinia, however, lies beyond the temporal bounds of the epic, and in place of that regular and fertile marriage Virgil thrusts before us images of perverted or sterile marriage that confuse the spheres of life and death. The tragic conceit of the wedding-as-funeral (e.g. Antigone as the bride of death) is evoked by Juno when she looks to Allecto to give Lavinia a dowry of Trojan and Italian blood (*Aen.* 7.313–22). In one of Virgil's disturbing images of uncontrolled female sexuality, Allecto's pullulating fertility of evil disrupts Latinus' plans for the succession. Earlier at Carthage the union of Aeneas and Dido (which would have produced the *wrong* dynasty) is sealed in an elemental and demonic parody of the Roman marriage ceremony (4.165–8). Marital stability in the *Aeneid* is achieved through a deficiency rather than an excess of physical sexuality: Andromache's fidelity to her dead husband Hector in her own version of an afterlife in this life,[3] and the final immutability of Dido's reunion with her former husband Sychaeus in death, the one example in the poem of lastingly reciprocated love (6.473–4).

---

[2] For the two lines, see O'Hara (1990), 144–7.   [3] See pp. 16–17 above.

From Virgil the line may be traced, for example, to Lucan's version of wedding-as-funeral in *Bellum Ciuile* 2.326–91. Cato, representative of the Roman Republic, is joined in remarriage with his former wife Marcia, fresh from the tomb of her second husband Hortensius to whom Cato had given her after she had provided him with the requisite three sons. In contrast to the fertility of the first marriage, this second wedding is a sterile and sexless reunion; the bride wears the funeral weeds in which she had lamented Hortensius, and this marriage will survive the couple's decease not through children but through the commemorative words on the wife's tomb, 'Marcia wife of Cato' (2.343–4). At the beginning of the next book the image of Marcia, pious inhabitant of the grave in this life, is inverted in the Fury-like apparition of the dead Julia, Pompey's first wife and daughter of Julius Caesar, who returns from the grave to haunt her former husband and remind him constantly that the relationship of son-in-law to father-in-law lives on with a Hellish vitality in the civil war between Pompey and Caesar. In Valerius' *Argonautica* the union of Jason and Medea, which was to end in an orgy of child-killing, is narrated through dense allusion to the Virgilian scenes of marital and sexual negativity; there is a master-stroke of irony and prolepsis in the simile at 7.401–2 that compares the fateful meeting of Jason and Medea at night in the grove of Hecate to the appearance of blind voiceless shades in the depths of the Underworld, an allusion to the condition of Dido (and Sychaeus) in the infernal afterword to the affair of Aeneas and Dido (*Aen.* 6.473–4).

The dynastic principle

Politics and families are always inseparable in Rome. That link assumes a new importance with the coming of the principate and the necessity for dynastic succession. In the *Aeneid* the figure in whom this concern centres is the son of Aeneas, Ascanius, whose other name Iulus is *the* dynastic name *par excellence*. Aeneas succeeds Hector as the bearer of Trojan hope for the future, and with that succession goes the replacement of Astyanax by Ascanius as the essential link between the present generation of heroes and the heroes and rulers of the future: Iulus is the eponymous ancestor of the *gens Iulia*. In other words Ascanius must repeat the success of Telemachus in surviving long enough to become a self-sufficient warrior and head of household like his father. In the *Aeneid* the equivalent of the Telemachy of *Odyssey* 1–4 is book 9, when Aeneas is

absent from the Trojan camp and Ascanius must weather Turnus'
fiercest assault on the survivors of Troy without the support of his father.
The scene in which he shoots dead the Italian braggart Remulus
Numanus and is then congratulated by Apollo (9.621–58) functions as a
rite de passage, in which Ascanius makes the passage from boy to man;
there are echoes of the highly symbolic passage at *Odyssey* 21.118–35
where Telemachus proves himself able to string his father's bow. But
Ascanius' coming of age is curiously qualified: Apollo forbids him from
further intervention in battle, and when we last see Ascanius in *Aeneid*
12.432–40, as Aeneas takes his leave for the final duel with Turnus, he
seems to have reverted to being a boy, whose complete learning of the
role of manhood (*uir-tus*) still lies in the future. In book 9 the (partial)
success of Ascanius is contrasted with the total failure of the young Nisus
and Euryalus to succeed and survive, youthful huntsmen whose first
essay in real warfare leads to their deaths.

Nisus and Euryalus are two of a series of young people in the *Aeneid*
who die tragically before their time – Pallas, Lausus, Camilla, and also
Dido and Turnus. These deaths are often interpreted as a mark of Virgil's
sympathy for suffering humanity, and even of his antipathy towards the
political goals of the principate. There may be some truth in that; but the
theme of the tragic death of the young, when taken together with the role
of Ascanius, also points to a more positive concern for, and commitment
to, the chances of success for Augustus' new order, still a young and
fragile affair in the 20s B.C.[4] This anxiety is focused above all in the scene
of Marcellus that concludes the Parade of Heroes in *Aeneid* 6. Here the
themes of family tradition and dynastic succession intersect: the
description of the young Marcellus who died in 23 B.C. is preceded by the
vision of his great ancestor, the Marcellus who won the *spolia opima* from
the Gaulish leader Virdomarus and who captured Syracuse during the
Second Punic War. Anchises has no doubt that had he survived the
second Marcellus would have more than lived up to his ancestor's
exploits. Note the stress on the name at 6.883 'you will be Marcellus' *tu
Marcellus eris*: everything is said in that conjunction of cognomen and
predicative use of 'to be'. But the supreme tragedy in his early death lay
for Augustus in the fact that he was marked out as successor to the
princeps. Critics who stress the 'private voice' of Virgil sometimes
overlook the fact that *this*, climactic, example of youthful death was the
result of illness, and not a life sacrificed to a military or political goal.

[4] See O'Hara (1990), 167–70.

The fragility and tenuousness of generational and dynastic continuity is at the heart of the Virgilian melancholy; the distance between Aeneas and Augustus, and the many further tests of survival that Aeneas' descendants will have to undergo *after* Ascanius–Iulus, create a sense of difficulty and uncertainty that cannot have been dissociated from the Augustan reader's sense of the future history of Rome after Augustus, for all that Virgil attempts to forestall such anxiety with images of the Golden Age, and so on. As Virgil may have divined, the question of dynastic succession was to be perhaps the single most acute problem for the survival of the principate through the first century A.D. When the body of the empire is indistinguishable from the mortal body of the emperor, the dissolution of the mortal frame of the one supreme man, the *unus homo* who holds *omnia*, may all too easily entail the disintegration of the body politic, resulting in a renewed plunge into the civil war out of which the principate had emerged. Seen in this light the line of epicists after Virgil is fuelled by the continuation in Roman historical reality of the conflict between Iliadic discontinuity and Odyssean continuity, a conflict that receives at best a tentative resolution in the *Aeneid*.

The themes of generational continuity and political power are often closely intertwined in the imperial epic. The civil wars of the dying Republic were frequently represented through the myth, no doubt all too often a reality, of strife within the family: the supreme example is the conflict between Caesar and Pompey, father-in-law and son-in-law, while a more generally available image is that of fratricide, with the particularly nasty variation of twin fratricide. In civil war the orderly succession of generations through father and son is cut off by mutual destruction within one generation. In the *Aeneid*, besides the succession motif embodied in Ascanius, there is the negative image of war between two kings whom fate has marked out already as father-in-law and son-in-law, Latinus and Aeneas. In the final duel between Turnus and Aeneas there is a far-reaching effacing of moral distinctions that suggests that the two are 'brothers' in their blind blood-lust;[5] ironically it is Turnus' appeal to their shared experience of what it is to be a son and to have a father that leads, through Aeneas' identification with Pallas, to his own annihilation. This is a starkly negative reworking of the finale of the otherwise tragic *Iliad* where the reconciliation between Priam and Achilles that is effected through Priam's appeal to Achilles' human

[5] See pp. 22–3 above.

feelings for his own father provides a temporary pause in the relentless slaughter of sons and fathers that will continue to the sack of Troy and beyond.

Ovid, for all the individual stories of family violence in the *Metamorphoses*, largely avoids putting the theme of generational continuity at the centre of his poem. Transformation paradoxically allows Ovid to sidestep the biological fact that the only kind of perpetuity lies in the replacement of one generation by the next, through another kind of stability: metamorphosis is an event that leads out of the world of change into a surreal world of unchanging forms that one may identify with the world as created by the poet. The Speech of Pythagoras at the end of the *Metamorphoses* describes a world of perpetual change, a philosophical view of mutability that is quite different from the poetic fantasy of metamorphosis into a fixed form. But Pythagorean metempsychosis itself provides an alternative model for the survival of the species to the familiar succession of mortal generations. Ovid's final self-apotheosis in the epilogue to the poem is an escape even from this more exotic kind of generational continuity, as he effects a final severance of his identity from his mortal body through the immortality of his poetry. When the poet is reduced to his name, a word whose only substance is the poetry, words, attached to that name, then at last the name, an empty sign detached from this or that living human instantiation, is charged with the fullness of an immutable and eternal being.

After the inversions of the *Metamorphoses* the Virgilian themes are replayed in more straightforward ways. Lucan describes a struggle for control of Rome, which is also a contest for mastery of the world and even universe, and at the same time is a struggle within families: between the father-in-law and son-in-law, Caesar and Pompey, and recurrently between brothers. The vision is entirely negative: this is a war from which there will be no resurrection through the continuity of generations (although the *name* of 'Caesar' will survive as 'a sign whose referent can shift forward through the principates here and there in the poem').[6] In *Aeneid* 6 the descent to the Underworld becomes a triumphal vision of life to come. The Parade of Heroes suggests the procession of the *imagines* of the ancestors at the funerals of great families, an institution that both commemorates the dead and celebrates the continued vitality

[6] Stephen Hinds *per litteras*.

94

of the *gens* through generation after generation. In Lucan the themes of funeral and *katabasis* tell only of extinction or degeneration.[7]

Statius intensifies the Lucanian focus by reverting to the archetypal legend of civil war and fratricide, the war between the brothers Polynices and Eteocles for power in Thebes. In a moralizing outburst at 1.142–64 Statius dwells on the insignificant stakes in this primitive civil war, nothing more than the poor city of Thebes, as opposed to later conflicts when the prize might be fabulous riches or an empire reaching to the ends of the earth. The sole motive was 'naked power' *nuda potestas* (1.150): 'power without wealth', but also 'power that is sufficient to itself' (like 'unadorned virtue' *nuda uirtus*). Statius' comment here is incongruous with our experience as we read through this hyperbolical epic, telling of a war which becomes every bit as cosmic as those of Lucan or Silius. Strife within the family turns into a battleground of Heaven and Hell. But by examining the Roman experience in the laboratory of a materially deprived Thebes, Statius strips bare the moving cause of the imperial epic, the desire for power, fuelled by the basic epic emotion anger (1.155 'how far do you stretch your anger?' *quo tenditis iras?* – anger being an inherently expansive and unlimited emotion). It is an emotion that obliterates the more orderly perpetuation and extension of power through blood-lines. Valerius Flaccus describes a journey imposed on the young Jason by a tyrant fearful of being overthrown, and the action both in Colchis and later is much concerned with power-succession and with problems within the family.

In Silius the emphasis within the theme of succession is placed more on the city (or state) than on the family, by a realization of what in the *Aeneid* is a matter for prophecy and allegory, the struggle between Rome and Carthage for mastery of the world. This is an episode in a larger history of the succession of empires: the Virgilian Jupiter hints at a *translatio imperii* from Greece to Rome, a theme taken up by Jupiter at greater length in Valerius' *Argonautica* when he explains to the Sun the place of the *Argo* in his grand scheme for the transfer of empire from Asia to Greece, and from Greece to 'other peoples' (1.531–60). In the mouth of Pythagoras in *Metamorphoses* 15.431–52 the place of Rome as the final empire in the succession becomes questionable; when change is king, what guarantee that Rome will be the exception that proves eternal?

[7] But here too Lucan exploits a negative undercurrent in the Virgilian Parade of Heroes, which contains a number of examples of 'sons falling short of their fathers' standards' (Feeney (1986b), 12).

Generational continuity in Silius is a theme that plays alongside the story of succession to empire rather than being tightly interwoven as in Lucan and Statius. The conflict between Carthage and Rome is to a large extent a war between the families of Hannibal and of Scipio Africanus. Book 1 stresses the role of Hannibal as successor to a long-standing hatred of Carthage for Rome, 'a war handed down to grandsons' *mandata nepotibus arma* (1.18). Hannibal's father Hamilcar dictates to the boy Hannibal an oath by the shade of Dido to persecute the Romans, marking a succession both to the natural father and to the remote national ancestor. Hannibal soon takes on his father's role in a more concrete way, when the Spanish army unanimously acclaims him successor as general to the murdered Hasdrubal, who had taken over the command when Hamilcar fell in battle. Before setting off to cross the Pyrenees and Alps into Italy, Hannibal attempts to define his own son's role as future successor to his father's and grandfather's military achievements (3.69–86). The Virgilian model is Aeneas' final address to Ascanius at *Aeneid* 12.435–40; but there is also a Homeric model, Hector's leave-taking of his wife and son in *Iliad* 6, which casts an ominous shadow over the scene. At the end of book 4, after the battles of Ticinus and Trebia, Hannibal receives an embassy from Carthage informing him that his son has been chosen by lot as one of the children selected annually for human sacrifice, a practice instituted by Dido (4.763–829). Out of fear and respect for their general the Carthaginian senate breaks with religious tradition by referring the final decision to Hannibal rather than to the lottery, which is to say to the gods. Hannibal accepts his position of equality with the gods in making the decision, and, reaffirming his son's destiny as successor to himself, attempts to placate the gods with the alternative of human victims in the forthcoming battle of Trasimene. The claim of 'Hannibal made equal with the gods' *Hannibal aequatus superis* (4.810), is presumptuous madness. Although the son is spared, the episode marks a symbolic devotion of the line of Hannibal to the Underworld.[8] Ironically it is Dido who, as founder of ritual child murder, is indirectly responsible: it is as if the spirit of Hell which set Hannibal off on his mock-Herculean labour is calling him and his family back to herself.

Scipio, on the other hand, finds in the Underworld a source of positive power. Book 13 marks a new beginning in the *Punica* after the climactic

---

[8] On the sacrificial aspects of this episode, see pp. 50–1.

failure of Hannibal to take Rome in book 12; the last five books stand as a kind of *Scipiad* with the emergence of Africanus as the last and greatest of Rome's leaders in the war. Like Hannibal, he is powered by contact with the Underworld, but Scipio re-enacts the pious descent of Aeneas to see the ghosts of his father (and uncle), marking the continuity between generations and the re-embodiment of the living virtues of the father in the son.[9] Book 13 sets the seal on a theme of Scipionic vigour and promise preserved that first emerges in book 4 in the account of Africanus' rescue of his father during the battle of Ticinus (4.401–79). A context is given by the preceding episode, the mutual slaughter of three Carthaginian and three Italian brothers. It is stressed that the two pairs are 'equal in age and spirit' (4.368); this is one of those mirror combats whose limiting case is the fratricide of civil war, and which forecloses the future through the extirpation of the present generation. For an epitaph Silius appropriates Virgil's lines on the death of Nisus and Euryalus (*Pun.* 4.396–400; cf. *Aen.* 9.446–9). Nisus and Euryalus, as we have seen, form a negative foil to the exploits of Ascanius in *Aeneid* 9, and it is as an Ascanius that Africanus is praised by Mars in words echoing those of Apollo to Ascanius (*Pun.* 4.472–7; cf. *Aen.* 9.641–4, 653–6). Silius 'improves' on Virgil: where Ascanius' first victory was the slaughter of an enemy, the boy Scipio's first 'victory' is the rescue of a father (4.429): Scipio repeats Aeneas' shouldering of Anchises out of the flames of Troy as he carries his own wounded father out of battle (4.466–71). It is proper that this paragon of filial piety and successful successor to family virtue should also be the opponent after Cannae of the *degener* (10.422) Metellus' proposal to abandon Rome and transfer the Roman survivors overseas (10.426–48).

Statius' *Thebaid*, like Lucan's *Bellum Ciuile*, dwells preponderantly on the negative theme of generations cut off, as one hero after another is killed off in a kind of epic *Ten Green Bottles*. In the case of Creon's son Menoeceus in book 10 it is an all too successful realization of family characteristics that leads to the extinction of the family's hopes: the goddess Virtue and the grieving father both recognize in Menoeceus' readiness to devote himself on the city's behalf the courage of Mars, for Menoeceus is the youngest of the race that sprang from the teeth of the

---

[9] The appearance, as in *Aeneid* 6, of the paired ghosts of Pompey and Caesar at *Pun.* 13.861–7 yields in Virgil and Silius a contrast with, respectively, Aeneas' and Scipio's piety. Silius describes Caesar as (863–4) 'Trojan Caesar descended from Iulus' as if to rebuke this destroyer of families with the family continuity to which he owes his very existence.

dragon of Mars (10.662–3, 806–9).[10] Perhaps the most pathetic of the Statian dead youths is Parthenopaeus, who combines features of Virgil's Nisus and Euryalus, Pallas and Camilla, and, in inversion, of Ascanius.[11] Statius' liking for the theme may have been one of the reasons for his subsequent choice of Achilles as hero of an epic; certainly the description of the boy Achilles in the completed section of the *Achilleid* bears strong similarities to the earlier Parthenopaeus.

The poet as successor/the successful poet

In a brilliant article entitled 'Allusion: The Poet as Heir'[12] Christopher Ricks discusses the self-referential quality of much allusion in English Augustan poetry, where allusion alludes to itself by taking as its reference models which have as their subject a relation of dependence: echo, reflection, paternity, succession. Several of his examples concern allusion to classical authors, for example (212):

> . . . the Virgilian allusion in one of Dryden's best poems, 'To the Memory of Mr. Oldham':

> > Once more, hail and farewel; farewel thou young,
> > But ah too short, *Marcellus* of our Tongue.   (lines 22–3)

> Dryden's translation of the *Aeneid* had discussed different interpretations of the lines at the end of Book 6:

> > 'Tis plain, that *Virgil* cannot mean the same *Marcellus*; but one of his Descendants; whom I call a new *Marcellus*; who so much resembled his Ancestor, perhaps in his Features, and his Person, but certainly in his Military Vertues, that *Virgil* cries out, *quantum instar in ipso est*! which I have translated, *How like the former, and almost the same.* –

> > > His Son, or one of his Illustrious Name,
> > > How like the former, and almost the same.

> > > > > (*Aeneid* 6. 1194–5)

> The beauty and propriety of the Virgilian allusion in 'To the Memory of Mr. Oldham' derive from the gentle confidence that to Virgil, Dryden would be 'one of his Descendants'.

---

[10] On the self-sacrifice of Menoeceus, see Hardie (1993b).
[11] See Hardie (1990b), 9–14.   [12] Ricks (1976).

Ricks also points to the parallelism between the concerns of Augustan poets as literary heirs and the contemporary importance in the social and political worlds of the issues of primogeniture and succession, 'in an era when kingship was a pondering of succession' (218).

The self-referentiality of classical allusions such as the one above to the end of *Aeneid* 6 extends to a larger structural parallel between the subject-matter and poetics of the English Augustans and those of the ancient poets, in particular writers of epic. The Roman imperial epic's obsession with the need for, and possibility of, succession reflects the historical realities of the first century A.D.; it also relates to the poet's own desire to prove himself a worthy successor to the great epic poets who lived before him, and in particular to succeed as a follower of Virgil. This intimate connection between epic subject matter and epic poetics may also be understood as a sharpening of a feature present in the genre from its beginning: the theme of generational continuity in the Homeric poems corresponds to the need of the oral tradition to preserve itself from extinction by ensuring that there is always a new generation of bards to repeat and renew the poems. This need found institutional expression in the Homerids of Chios, a guild of rhapsodes who claimed to be the descendants of Homer and who regarded themselves as the guardians of the Homeric poems.

The epic poet is supposed to be objective, an impartial recorder of the memorials of heroic deeds in the past, the dutiful mouthpiece of the Muses. Recent criticism of Roman epic, in particular of Ovid's *Metamorphoses* and Lucan's *Bellum Ciuile*, has powerfully demonstrated a conspiratorial collusion between the epic poet and the characters and actions of his narrative; epic poets turn out to be anything but disinterested. Before looking in greater detail at the epic's treatment of epic succession it will be helpful to survey the evidence for the claim that, long before the self-consciousness of an Ovid, the epic poet had already embedded himself deeply in his own epic narrative.

Epic poet and epic hero

From the beginning hero and poet are joined symbiotically in a common purpose, the creation of *kleos*, 'glory' or 'fame', the hero through the performance of memorable deeds, the poet through the commemoration of those deeds. Beyond this, epic heroes themselves feel a strong pressure to narrate, by telling stories of past heroic exploits, as Odysseus most famously does in the *Odyssey*, but as do Nestor, Phoenix and others too. The hero may even take the bard's lyre into his own hands, as Achilles does to while away the time that he is absent from the war by singing of the 'famous deeds of heroes' (*Iliad* 9.186–9). Hermann Fränkel writes suggestively of the convergence in the *Odyssey* between the figure of Odysseus, the master of fictions who must approach the table of the great as an outsider begging for favours, and the presumed reality of life for a typical bard, under the necessity of filling his belly by singing songs to please kings at their feasts.[13] Odysseus' stringing of the bow, the climactic proof of the hero's continuing potency, is compared in a simile to the stringing of a lyre by the bard (*Odyssey* 21.406–8). The *Odyssey* also includes direct portraits of more or less idealized bards (Phemius and Demodocus), with specimens of their art.[14]

Successful epic poets are treated by posterity in much the same way that they themselves treat the heroes of whom they sing: the bard too is heroized, or even divinized, and the immortal fame that he bestows on his characters becomes his own. The epic hero is a model of virtue to be imitated, even if it is granted that men in those days were inherently greater than men of the present day. The heroic grandeur of a Homer challenges imitation at the same time as it creates the fear of inferiority.

Virgil brings the analogy between bard and hero up to date by a bold claim for the similarity between achievement of poet and *princeps*.[15] This equation is made explicitly in the proem of the third *Georgic*, where Virgil uses the licence of Hesiodic self-advertisement to announce the forth-coming appearance of his epic on the achievements of Octavian and his ancestors. Virgil will celebrate the triumphs of the *princeps* in the only adequate kind of poetry, that of a poetic *triumphator*, as he leads the Muses of Helicon in his triumphal procession to the banks of the river of Mantua. This image of poetic triumph suggests success in a competition with other poets, past or present; it also hints at appropriation and succession, appropriation of the poetic goods of others as personified in the Muses, and succession in that this is another in a series of triumphs (*Geo.* 3.8–9): 'I must attempt a path on which I *also* may raise myself from the ground and wing my victorious way on the lips of men'. Virgil is to imitate the success of other great poets, in the first place Ennius whose epitaph is alluded to in these lines. But the '*also*' may be interpreted

---

[13] Fränkel (1975), 10–11.

[14] Further discussion (with references) of the inscription of the poet in the Homeric texts in Goldhill (1991), 56–68.   [15] See Buchheit (1972).

retrospectively when we read through to the end of the last book of the poem and find the great Caesar winning victories in the East and 'making his way to Olympus' (4.562). In this proud claim to equality with the first man of Rome may be traced not only Hesiod's boast that the Muse Calliope is the companion of kings (as well as poets) (*Theog.* 79–93), but also Lucretius' transference of the image of triumph from the victorious general to the intellectual conqueror Epicurus (1.72–9),[16] and hence by implication to Lucretius' own performance as poetic imitator of Epicurus, and to the performance of the competent reader of the *De rerum natura*. If the Homeric tradition already allowed complicity between the poet and his characters, Virgil's close engagement with Lucretius further eased the possibility of slippage between the roles of epic poet, epic characters and readers of epic. The shared experience of poet, characters and readers of *Paradise Lost* is closely analogous in its working to the *De rerum natura*, and may argue for a direct use of Lucretius by Milton.

Virgil's association of the roles of military man and poet finds another reflex in the line of warrior-priests and warrior-poets who die in battle,[17] starting with Cretheus in the *Aeneid*, 9.774–7, who sang of *arma uirum*. Statius seems to be responsible for the neat encapsulation of the Virgilian theme of the poet triumphant in the image of the two laurels, those of the general and poet.[18] Claudian gives us the fiction of an Ennius always at the side of the conquering Scipio, and winning the wreath of the laurel of Mars in a victory that brought back the Muses to Rome.[19] Statius and Claudian showed Petrarch the way to the joint triumph of Scipio and Ennius with which Petrarch's epic *Africa* concludes; Petrarch's staging of his own laureation on the Capitol in 1341 is the dramatic realization of a script that is at least as old as Virgil's poetic triumph in the third *Georgic*.[20]

Poetic succession

There seems to be a strong pressure for epic poets to associate their own deaths with the deaths of their fictional heroes or with the destruction of

---

[16] Buchheit (1971).

[17] The priest is a common figure for the poet in ancient poetics: *uates* denotes both.

[18] *Achill.* 1.15–16 [Domitian] 'for whom the twin laurels of bard and general burgeon in mutual rivalry' (presumably to be taken as a positive example of Statian twin rivalry). [19] *Cos. Stilich.* 3 *praef.* [20] See Suerbaum (1972).

the poems themselves. Virgil's attempt to involve his unfinished *Aeneid* in his personal annihilation was stagily imitated by Ovid's claim that he tried to burn the *Metamorphoses* when he was banished to a living death in exile. Lucan's suicide was a self-consciously literary affair in the manner of the self-chosen deaths that litter the *Bellum Ciuile*; Silius like Lucan both wrote about, and acted out, the Stoic's voluntary exit from life under intolerable circumstances. There seems in this to be something more than ancient literary biography's habit of spinning out a poet's life from his works, although Petrarch's imagination was probably working overtime when he noted in his copy of Virgil against the last line of the *Aeneid* ('with a groan Turnus' life fled complaining to the shades'): 'you were too sure a prophet of your own death: for with such words on your lips life fled you'. Here I wish to examine the ways in which the poems yield models not for the poet's end but for his beginning.

Scenes of instruction and transmission figure prominently in the *Aeneid*, and in many cases a metapoetical symbolism lies close to the surface. Aeneas' part in the narrative of the *Aeneid* begins with his vision of the ghost of Hector telling him to flee from Troy with the gods of the city (*Aen.* 2.268–97). Several kinds of succession, of the past handing over to the future, are implied. Firstly, the hero who preserved Troy in the *Iliad* designates Aeneas as his successor to bear the future hopes of the Trojan race. Troy is lost, and Aeneas must seek new walls for the gods, the first of a series of cities succeeding Troy, the last of which will be Rome. Secondly, the hero of the *Iliad* hands over to the hero of the *Aeneid*, just as the Roman Virgil takes over the epic mantle from Homer. In general terms Aeneas' journey from east to west, which will ultimately involve not just the supersession of Troy but also reconciliation with, and then conquest of, Greece, bears an analogy to the naturalization of the epic on Italian soil by Virgil, as well as to more abstract kinds of passage that challenged a poet at Virgil's historical and cultural moment. R. M. Durling writes of the *Aeneid* 'Because of the element of learned imitation . . . the inspiration of the Poet is endangered and thematically crucial in Virgil; it is parallel to the dilemma of Aeneas, who must mediate between an intolerable past and a distant future by means of whatever elusive capacity for transcendent vision he possesses.'[21] Thirdly, the presence of Homer in Hector is also suggested by Virgil's imitation in this episode of the Dream of the shade of Homer with which Ennius opened his

---

[21] Durling (1965), 8. For similar reflections see Bono (1984), ch. 1.

Annals.[22] Virgil chooses not to follow Ennius' lead in beginning his epic with a lengthy and direct presentation of his own poetic persona in the manner of Hesiod or Callimachus; instead he displaces the poet's dream on to the hero of the poem, but retains a metapoetic reference to the poet's own place in a scheme of succession. The Ennian moment is as important as the Homeric: this is an allusion that alludes to itself, in Ricks' terms, for in alluding to Ennius' claim to be the successor of Homer the allusion enacts Virgil's own claim to be the modern successor of Ennius (as well as of Homer).

In Ennius' Dream at the beginning of the *Annals* a phantom of Homer explained to Ennius how the real soul of Homer was reincarnated in the breast of Ennius.[23] This Pythagoreanizing fiction is an extraordinarily confident version of epic succession; there is no sense of a struggle required to take over the old and make it one's own and new, nor is there even the distance involved in the natural succession of poetic son to father, but instead the limiting case of poetic identity: Ennius *is* Homer. This confidence will not be repeated in later Latin epicists with the exception of Ovid. Note further how uncannily Ennius opens the Latin hexameter epic tradition by attributing to the epic poet the impersonation, reincarnation or possession that so often seems to be the lot of the epic actors (see chapter 2).

Virgil alludes again to the Ennian Dream of Homer in the scene between Anchises and Aeneas in the Underworld in *Aeneid* 6.679–892.[24] The tears and words of Anchises on seeing his son echo the tears and words of the shade of Homer addressing Ennius, and the first part of the Speech of Anchises on the nature of the soul reworks Homer's Pythagorean account of the nature of the soul and the cycle of metempsychosis in Ennius. In the second, historical, part of his speech Anchises tells Aeneas of the succession of Alban and Roman kings, and of the generations of Roman heroes and warriors who will bridge the gap between Aeneas' forthcoming wars in Italy and the renewal of the Saturnian Golden Age under Augustus. The procession of heroes yet to

---

[22] See Austin on *Aen.* 2.271, 274. Petrarch brilliantly reverses Virgil's appropriation of the Ennian dream by adapting Aeneas' reaction to the mutilated form of Hector, 'alas what a sight he was' *ei mihi qualis erat* (*Aen.* 2.274), to Homer's presentation of himself to Ennius in his dream at the end of the *Africa*, 9.175 'behold the sight of Homer as he was once in his life' *aspice qualis erat quondam dum uixit Homerus.* Petrarch knew of Virgil's Ennian source from Servius.

[23] See Brink (1972), 556–65.   [24] See Hardie (1986), 69–83.

be born is an inversion of the Roman aristocratic funeral procession of the heroic ancestors of the past. Not all the heroes that Anchises shows to Aeneas are members of the Julian *gens*; but for this there was to be a close analogy in the funeral of Augustus himself, when the procession included impersonations not just of the *princeps'* own ancestors, but of other great Romans of the past as well. The principle of family succession, from father to son, has here been widened into a retrospective claim for political legitimation on the basis of the fiction that the dead emperor is the true 'son and heir' to all those great Romans of earlier times who served the state. It is the mirror image of the title of 'father of the fatherland' *pater patriae*, bestowed on Augustus by the Senate. This vision of the future history of Rome is the continuation of the successful succession from father to son narrated within the *Aeneid* in the persons of Anchises, Aeneas and Iulus. The son Aeneas is instructed by the dead father Anchises: through this contact with a past that preserves its vitality Aeneas is given strength to act in the present with an eye on fame in future ages (6.889). This is the Roman party-line on how public men should behave; it is also a close description of the conditions of literary production in Rome, above all of the writing of epic. The relationship between Aeneas and Anchises is also that between Virgil and 'father' Ennius. Ennian echoes continue in the historical part of the Speech of Anchises; the last line of the main catalogue of heroes (6.846) is a quotation of an Ennian line praising Fabius Cunctator, with the change of one word, as if to nail the Ennian nature of the speech.[25] The historical review of Roman heroes does of course cover, elliptically, the subject of Ennius' *Annals*. Virgil marks himself as the successor to Ennius in two ways: firstly, by placing the quotations of Ennius in the mouth of a character in his own epic Virgil, at one remove, appropriates them as his own words. Secondly, Anchises moves beyond the temporal limit of the *Annals* to survey the subsequent course of Roman history down to the time of Augustus and Virgil. For Virgil what Ennius narrates is unfinished business; it is his job through the medium of his legendary epic to map out the successful conclusion of the annals of Rome with the return of the Golden Age under Augustus. Further, this continuation of the *Annals* is doubly Ennian, for Ennius himself had later added three more books to the original fifteen.[26] Virgil's transformation of the

[25] See p. 5 above.
[26] As D. C. Feeney points out *per litteras*. Anchises' concluding Ennian quotation may hint at a further self-reflexivity: Virgil might aspire to be the unique poet who 'renewed' the epic subject-matter (*res*) of Ennius.

Homeric Underworld into a scene of poetic instruction and transmission was determinative for the practice of succeeding epicists of beginning their poems in a version of the Underworld, although after Lucan the charge from the depths is usually a negative one.[27]

The other major prophecy of future history in the middle of the *Aeneid*, the Shield of Aeneas at the end of book 8, also reveals the poet putting on the mask of Ennius but going beyond in a pious outdoing. The first scene on the Shield, the twins and the she-wolf, echoes Ennius closely, if Servius is to be believed.[28] Once more the survey of Roman history takes in Ennian subjects only to leap forward to the glorious achievements of Augustus. But even here Ennius is not rudely pushed to the side: the final scene of a triumphing *princeps* and a new temple of a god of military and poetic excellence, Apollo, probably alludes to the conclusion of the first edition of Ennius' *Annals*, the triumph in 187 B.C. of Ennius' patron Fulvius and the founding of the temple of Hercules and the Muses (probably also a model for Virgil's poetic triumph at the beginning of the third *Georgic*). The microcosmic Shield is a poetic icon: as well as an image of Roman history it is an image of the universe, reflecting the claim of Virgilian epic to be universal epic.[29] Its creator Vulcan is a figure of the Roman epic tradition and of Virgil's claim to embody that tradition in its most complete and omniscient form, a point made by the pun at 8.627 *haud uatum ignarus*, 'not unaware of the prophets', but also 'not unaware of the bards'.

The successors of Virgil

Of recent years there has been a growth industry in interpretations of the *Metamorphoses* that read figures of the poet into an apparently endless number of episodes:[30] to name the most obvious, Narcissus and Pygmalion as examples of the self-reflexive producer of images; the competitions between the Muses and the Pierides, and between Minerva and Arachne as narrative fictions of the programmatic literary debates of Alexandria and Augustan Rome; Orpheus appears in person to sing his own catalogue of transformations and erotic adventures. Ovidian

---

[27] See pp. 60–5 above.

[28] The scene of loving maternity may hint at Ennius' poetic paternity of Virgil, not Ennius' biological offspring any more than Romulus and Remus are the biological offspring of the she-wolf!   [29] Hardie (1986), ch. 8.

[30] E.g. Leach (1974); Rosati (1983); Hinds (1987); Solodow (1988), ch. 6; Harries (1990).

self-consciousness and self-reflexiveness are undoubtedly signs of the Hellenistic, Callimachean quality of the *Metamorphoses*; but consideration of the more orthodox epic tradition before and after Ovid should prevent the conclusion that these features mark a generic distinction between the *Metamorphoses* and Homeric or Virgilian epic.

As we have seen, the basic narrative motif of the *Metamorphoses*, transformation, replaces (transforms?) the traditional epic concern with succession in the family and state with another model of the interplay of continuity and discontinuity. At the end of the poem Ovid's confident claim to a future poetic immortality brushes aside anxieties about succession and success, but not before the Speech of Pythagoras, which functions as a foil to Ovid's own escape from mutability of all kinds, has cunningly and comprehensively rehearsed the key passages concerning succession in the earlier Latin epic tradition. This is a monumental example of Ricks' 'allusion that alludes to itself'. The starting-point is Ennius: Ovid's Pythagoras delivers a vastly expanded version of the Pythagoreanizing Speech of Homer in the Dream at the beginning of the *Annals*, an account of the nature of the universe and of the soul that preluded Ennius' narrative of the history of Rome. In Ovid a drastically truncated history of Rome also forms the climax to Pythagoras' disquisition on change (*Met.* 15.431–52), but the outline of the story is Virgilian rather than Ennian, the destruction of one city, Troy, as the prerequisite for the creation and eventual supremacy of another, Rome. Thus Ovid recognizes the *Aeneid*'s claim to be the successor to, and fulfiller of, Ennius' epic. Homer's speech to Ennius dramatizes the succession of Roman epic to Greek epic, as a prelude to the *Annals*. Ovid's Pythagoras provides a retrospective philosophical theory of change to test against the preceding fourteen books; his audience is the second Roman king, Numa, and the meeting between Greek philosopher and Roman statesman is another major (if fictional) episode in the transmission of Greek culture to Italy. Beyond these specific examples of succession, the Speech of Pythagoras is a more generalized comment on the pedigree of Roman epic, demonstrating that mutability and philosophy are not alien transplants by Ovid into that tradition. Repeated allusion to the hexameter philosophical poet Empedocles points to a source that flows to Ennius and to Lucretius, from both of whom streams then run into the *Aeneid* (again we are directed to the Speech of Anchises in *Aeneid* 6).

It has never been possible to ignore Lucan's involvement as narrator and spectator in his epic: the poet frequently apostrophizes his characters and expresses his own moral judgments on the monstrous events that he narrates. He comments directly on his own relation to his subject and to his poetic ancestry at 9.980–6, where he addresses Caesar at the site of Troy and assures him that he need not be prey to an envy of Homer's power to immortalize that troubled Alexander the Great on the occasion of his visit to the tomb of Achilles.[31] Lucan proudly claims for himself a fame as enduring as the 'honours' paid to Homer, and foretells for his poem the eternal life that Ovid looks forward to at the end of the *Metamorphoses*.[32] He also puts himself on a level with Caesar: 'coming ages will read *me and you*' (985), the poet and his hero as yoke-fellows, by a compression of the Ovidian insinuation that the poet's immortality is comparable to that of the deified Julius (or Augustus). But here poetic success is juxtaposed with the failure of the historical succession of empires. By dense allusion to the *Aeneid* the description of the deserted site of Troy becomes all too clearly an allegory of what Caesar is doing to Rome; this is an end to the perilously preserved transmission of power and family that has led from the Sack of Troy to the Roman empire. The ghost of Hector had handed over the future of Troy to Aeneas; Lucan's Caesar has to be prevented by an inhabitant of the site of Troy from 'trampling on the shade of Hector'. His unwitting violation of sacred places then leads him to blunder over the 'Hercean altar', violated once long before when Achilles' son slaughtered Priam there after killing his son Polites before his eyes. Rome succeeds Troy only as one shadow of a city succeeds another shadow in a sterile repetition; poetic vitality has become totally detached from political vitality.[33]

Recent criticism has dragged into the light the shadow of the epic poet Lucan lurking behind characters engaged in acts of prophecy and necromancy.[34] The frenzied matron whose apocalyptic visions close the first book of the *Bellum Ciuile* is inspired by Apollo, and compared to a Maenad filled with the god Bacchus, two gods considered (before being rejected) as sources of poetic inspiration by Lucan in the prologue of

[31] See p. 17 above.
[32] *Bell. Ciu.* 9.985–6 'men in coming ages will read me and thee; our Pharsalia will live' *uenturi me teque legent; Pharsalia nostra|uiuet; Met.* 15.878–9 'I shall be read on the lips of the people of the empire, and, if there be any truth in vatic forebodings, through all centuries I shall enjoy fame – I shall live' *ore legar populi, perque omnia saecula fama,|siquid habent ueri uatum praesagia, uiuam.*
[33] See p. 16 above.   [34] Masters (1992); O'Higgins (1988).

book 1. The *furor* that gives her no rest (1.681) is scarcely to be distinguished from the *furor* which impels the citizens of Rome to destroy themselves in civil war (1.8) and which also drives Lucan to compose the epic of that civil war. The major scenes of prophetic inspiration occur at the centre of the poem, in Appius' consultation of the Pythian priestess in book 5, and Sextus' visit to Erictho and Erictho's necromancy in book 6. Both episodes rework Aeneas' consultation of the Sibyl and interview with his dead father in *Aeneid* 6. In the two passages we may see aspects of Lucan's own poetic nature and inspiration scattered in fragments over the several actors involved: Appius, the Pythia Phemonoe, Apollo; Sextus, Erictho, the reanimated corpse. The fragmentation is itself a direct reflection of Lucan's awareness of the divisions within his own poetic being, as Masters brilliantly displays. In both cases there is a contrast between the enormous resources of power and knowledge hinted at, and the exiguous amount of information actually revealed. Both the Pythia and Erictho have at their disposal a complete grasp of history and time, a kind of ideal model of the universal epic and particularly close to the Ovidian version of that model,[35] but neither Appius nor Sextus is made a party to this totality.

In terms of the sources and vehicles for inspiration there is an analogous contrast between immediacy and discontinuity. The Pythia is invaded by Apollo, and the god, who has never been present more fully (*plenior* 5.166), completely replaces the human in the priestess' breast. Erictho is not content to call up ghosts, but instead brings the corpse itself back to life. But at Delphi this supreme example of possession comes as the passing revival of a tradition extinct; the oracle has been long silent (for centuries, Phemonoe implies), and presumably Phemonoe is the current office-holder in a succession that has for some time consisted of voiceless priestesses. This is in a sacred place famous for its succession of presiding deities (Aesch. *Eum.* 1–20), a tradition alluded to by Lucan in the introductory description of Delphi (*Bell. Ciu.* 5.79–85, here in the version that Apollo succeeded violently to Themis, as he comes violently to Phemonoe). Phemonoe's trance is her last; as she comes round she falls (5.224), apparently in the death foretold at 116–20. Likewise the reward for the corpse in book 6 is a return to death, that

---

[35] 5.179 *rerum series;* 6.612 *causarum series* – i.e. a version of the *perpetuum carmen* (1.70 *fatorum series*, after an echo of the first line of the *Metamorphoses* in 1.67 *fert animus causas*). Cf. also 5.181 *non prima dies, non ultima mundi* (*deerant*); 6.611 *a prima descendit origine mundi*, echoing *Met.* 1.3.

Erictho assures him will now be eternal (6.763–7). Masters comments (p. 138) 'in the *Bellum Ciuile* epic is resurrected and lives again a weird, grotesque afterlife, before it is allowed to die for good'. In the case of Erictho's corpse the break with any intelligible principle of succession to a past is clear through a comparison with the Virgilian model. The corpse takes the place of Anchises: instead of the father an unknown soldier, without past or future. Sextus prides himself on being 'the famous son of Pompey the Great' (6.594); the poet tells us that he is a degenerate, who does not live up to his father's name. It is proper that the worthless son of the great general should commune with one who is even more nameless than himself, one who is specified only as *Pompeiana umbra* (6.717), by which we may understand 'the ghost of a Pompeian' or 'a shadow of Pompey'. The Virgilian model would require that Sextus meet his father; the nameless soldier is the shadow of that expectation. In the *Bellum Ciuile* Pompey is already a shadow of his former self (1.135), and in the course of the narrative that 'shadow' will become a 'shade', one of the dead (8.841). The corpse's final message to Sextus is that he will obtain a more certain prophecy of the future from his father Pompey himself, in Sicily. *Ipse Pompeius* is heavily ironical (as the word *ipse* so often is in Latin epic): by the time that Sextus comes to Sicily his father will be long dead, and Sextus will at last fulfil the Virgilian role of living son meeting dead father – but now just a shadow of a shadow, not the man himself. This reunion of father and son will confirm only the extinction of the family line and of the future history of Rome: the end of success and succession. It is not surprising to find verbal echoes of Virgil's lament over Marcellus in the final words of Erictho's corpse.

Violence and death characterize Lucan's dealings with the past, as they are also the characteristic events of civil war. Lucan takes control of his predecessors' material not as a respectful son entering into a father's inheritance, but as a rebel, yet unable to escape from the paradigms and values of his society, which he angrily seizes for his own and reverses into a negative parody of themselves, galvanizing the words and forms of the past into a furious appearance of life whose subsidence leaves, apparently, only death.[36] But epic was not to 'die for good'. Nero's paroxysmic end led only to new versions of the principate; Lucan's *Bellum Ciuile* was succeeded by more imperial epics. Erictho's spells could not deliver the genre from later revivals.

[36] Cf. Greenblatt (1980), ch. 5 (on Marlowe), esp. 209.

Statius' epilogue to the *Thebaid* is a mixture of confident hope and modesty. In the *envoi* to the poem he reworks Ovidian topoi,[37] cautiously looking forward to the survival of his epic after its creator's death. But where Ovid implies a personal divinity on a par with that of the deified *princeps*, Statius warns his poem not to attempt to rival the 'divine *Aeneid*', but to 'follow at a distance and ever worship the *Aeneid*'s footsteps' (12.816–17). To follow is to imitate, which may in itself demand exertion, as for example in the case of Hylas trying to keep up with Hercules at 5.441–4 'walking boldly Hylas follows in the footsteps of great Hercules, and, despite Hercules' lumbering bulk, he hardly keeps up with him at a run; he carries the Lernaean arms and delights to sweat under the huge weight of the quiver',

> audet iter magnique sequens uestigia mutat
> Herculis et tarda quamuis se mole ferentem
> uix cursu tener aequat Hylas Lernaeaque tollens
> arma sub ingenti gaudet sudare pharetra.

Virgil himself, when charged with plagiarism, had said that it was easier to steal the club of Hercules than a line from Homer.[38] Statius' respectful distance from Virgil here contrasts with Calliope's prophecy to the infant Lucan in Statius' birthday poem in honour of the dead Lucan (*Siluae* 2.7), that (79–80) 'the *Aeneid* itself will worship you when you sing to the Latins', *ipsa te Latinis|Aeneis uenerabitur canentem*. Even allowing for the conventions of panegyric, there may be in this a recognition of Lucan's immodest challenge to the authority of Virgil. Statius' own attitude to the *Aeneid* may rather be compared with that of Silius, paying his respects to the tomb of Virgil and celebrating his birthday. Reverence of the god and following in his footsteps are also the images used by Lucretius to define his relationship to his *philosophical* model, 'father' Epicurus; this is in sharp contrast to the adversarial pose that Lucretius takes up towards cultural and poetic idols, including notably Ennius, the pose which is then naturalized by Virgil in the epic in his imitation and criticism of Lucretius, and so handed down to Ovid and Lucan. The Lucretian model of philosophical imitation provides one key to the interpretation of the Statian statement: the reader who successfully follows Lucretius' poem will, in so doing, also follow the footsteps of Epicurus and arrive at the same destination, a godlike state of imperturbability. Just so the *Thebaid*'s successful imitation of the *Aeneid* may result in a measure of self-divinization. And indeed the last two lines

---

[37] *Am.* 3.15.19–20; *Tr.* 3.7.49–54; *Met.* 15.878–9.   [38] *Vita Donati* 46.

of the *Thebaid* seem to hint at this; Statius looks to a time in the future, after his death, when Envy evaporates and the poem will be accorded its 'deserved honours' (*meriti honores* 819). The language is that of worship paid to a god or hero,[39] the language that Silius uses in his canonization of Ennius (see below). Even if Statius advises his poem for the present to follow at a distance, the future holds *honores* that might well be those of a god. The explicit statement of the poet may not of course coincide with his poetic practice, and Statius does not always succeed in suppressing the Lucanian aspects of his poem, if that was his intention.

In terms of political power the *Thebaid*, like the *Bellum Ciuile*, tells only of succession perverted and thwarted. But there is in the narrative a model for successful succession, when the Argive force has to choose a successor[40] to Amphiaraus after the warrior-prophet (a *uates*) has been swallowed by the earth (8.271–341). The unanimous choice to take up the laurel of prophecy is Thiodamas, the son of Melampus who had been the aged partner of Amphiaraus in prophetic skill in the scene of augury in book 3. Amphiaraus has been cut off in his prime, and his own family has one of the more lurid histories in Greek mythology; the young Thiodamas represents a kind of spiritual son. Already while alive Amphiaraus had shared the secrets of the gods with Thiodamas, 'and rejoiced to hear him called his like and close second', (8.282 *gaudebat dici similem iuxtaque secundum*). Thiodamas is as bashful about his position as Statius is with regard to Virgil (284 'he humbly worships the prophetic leaves offered to him' *oblatas frondes submissus adorat*). In a simile he is compared to an Achaemenian prince, a 'boy', who succeeds to the Persian throne on the untimely death of the king and feels himself incapable of filling his father's shoes (8.286–93). The setting is exotic, but the problems might be Roman; it may be tact on Statius' part to avoid a direct comparison with the imperial succession, or there may be a hint that they do these things better in barbarian lands.[41]

---

[39] *meriti honores* for a god: *Aen.* 3.118, 264; 8.189. *refero* 'to render (honours to a deity or hero)' *OLD* 13c. *mox* of future apotheosis: *Geo.* 1.24.

[40] *Theb.* 8.276 'who should work the tripods as successor': for *successor* in the context of poetic succession see Ov. *Tr.* 4.10.53–5 '[Tibullus] was your successor, Gallus, and Propertius his; in order of time I myself was the fourth, and as I worshipped my predecessors, so my followers worshipped me'. For Amphiaraus as a figure of the epic poet see Henderson (1991), 66 n. 44, 69 n. 73.

[41] Along the lines of Horace *Odes* 3.24.9 'the Scythians do things better' (than the Romans). There may be a hint of a similar contrast when Theseus returns from his successful taming of the Scythians (12.519 ff.) to find savagery rampant in Greece (12.591–3).

Thiodamas gives a first earnest of his priestly powers with the Lucretian prayer to *Tellus*, ending with an address to Amphiaraus in which he claims that *Natura* has swallowed him 'as if she were entombing him in the Cirrhaean chasm' (*Theb.* 8.331), that is, as a source of potent prophetic subterranean inspiration like that at Delphi.[42] For Thiodamas Amphiaraus will be an alternative god of prophecy to Apollo (336), a substitution that suggests Lucretius' location in philosophical reason of more reliable 'oracular' sources than Apollo;[43] he concludes by paying Amphiaraus the honour of funeral rites. Day has broken and the army moves to battle; the Spartan contingent has not yet reconciled itself to the loss of its old leader and the succession of the new (366 *necdum accessere regenti*). Thiodamas does not enter fully into his inheritance until the final night of the war in book 10, after the Argives have suffered the further loss of Tydeus, Hippomedon and Parthenopaeus. At this low point Thiodamas is inspired to urge his fellows to nocturnal slaughter of the Thebans. The narrator speculates that the inspiring god may be Juno or Apollo (10.162–3). Thiodamas himself has more certain information: he tells the Argive captains 'these words come not from my own breast: the voice is his whom your trust forced me to serve and to put on his fillets, and he himself was of the same mind'

> . . . non hae de nostro pectore uoces:
> ille canit, cui me famulari et sumere uittas
> uestra fides, ipso non discordante, subegit. (189–91)[44]

He is just a mouthpiece (*pro-phetes*) or mask through which the true voice of Amphiaraus speaks. This is a normal model of prophetic inspiration (Statius has in mind in particular the possession of the Virgilian Sibyl by Apollo), but it is unusual in that the possessing divinity is the mortal prophet's own human predecessor in the art. Thiodamas then reports the nocturnal epiphany of Amphiaraus in a scene of admonition and instruction based on Aeneas' vision of the ghost of Hector in *Aeneid* 2.[45] Aeneas exclaims 'alas, what a sight he was' *ei mihi, qualis erat* (*Aen.*

---

[42] Cf. Lucan 5.86–96.

[43] Lucr. 1.736–9 'Through their many excellent and divine discoveries they, as it were, delivered responses from their heart's shrine that were far more sacred and sure than the prophecies that the Pythian priestess utters from Apollo's tripod and laurel' (1.738–9 = 5.111–12). Note also Lucan 1.63–6: Apollo is superfluous if Nero is the Muse.

[44] The possession is as powerful as that of Lucan's Phemonoe by Apollo, but there had been little *concordia* in that episode.   [45] See pp. 102–3 above.

2.274), marking the difference between the mangled form of Hector and his former glory; Thiodamas also uses *qualis erat* (*Theb.* 10.204), but to tell us that Amphiaraus is 'as he was'; unlike Hector he has suffered no diminution in appearance – or potence – on leaving the world above. The words *qualis erat* were very likely also found in Virgil's Ennian model, applied to the sorry appearance of the shade of the dead Homer.[46] In the *Aeneid* Hector in effect designates Aeneas as a surrogate for his own dead son; Amphiaraus reminds Thiodamas of his duty to live up to his father when he uses the word *degener* (209) to rebuke him. By his present performance Thiodamas demonstrates that he is not a disgrace to his father Melampus.

In Thiodamas Statius presents a model of an ideal succession and of an inspiration in which there is a total communication of clarity and energy from the dead to the living. Not a pale shadow of Amphiaraus, but the man himself, *ipse, ipse* (10.203),[47] Thiodamas assures his audience. It was the wraith of Homer that appeared in a dream to Ennius, but to reveal to him that the real Homer still lived in the breast of the Latin poet. Statius uses Ennian and Lucretian models of an ideal transmission of poetic, philosophical or prophetic insight, to suggest a healing of the painful ruptures in communication that characterize the instances of necromancy and prophecy in Lucan; Amphiaraus, the man who has descended to the Underworld while still alive, reads as a positive version of Erictho's living corpse – or of Statius' own exemplar of life in death, Oedipus.

Silius uses the privilege of his historical subject to introduce both Homer and Ennius in person to his narrative; both poetic predecessors are written into scenes of succession taken from Silius' most important predecessor, Virgil.[48] Ennius appears as a centurion fighting in the Sardinian campaign in *Punica* 12.387–419. As one of the warrior-poets in the Virgilian tradition the father of Latin epic literally takes part in his own subject-matter, the history of the Second Punic War (there is no evidence that the real Ennius actually wrote himself into his *Annals*). Silius wishes (12.390) to 'sanctify the bard with the honours that he deserves' *meritum uati sacremus honorem*; the phrase *meriti honores* is used of offerings to the gods in Virgil, and is the reward that Statius expects for himself at the end of the *Thebaid*. These divine honours Silius here pays directly by celebrating the deeds of Ennius as godlike hero, but

---

[46] *Ann.* 442 Skutsch.
[47] Always with the proviso that in epic the word *ipse* is often not quite itself.
[48] On Silius' relation to Virgil, see pp. 64–5 above.

also more generally by according him the honour of imitation, just as Virgil is in real life honoured as a god and imitated by Silius. Ennius encounters the Sardinian Hostus, the virtuous son of a barbaric father, Hampsagoras, who boasts of Trojan ancestors (12.344–7). Hostus represents the future hopes of this proud family, and himself looks for eternal fame by killing Ennius (12.403). Father and son constitute a barbaric double of those Italian families like the *gens Iulia* whom Virgil celebrates in the *Aeneid*; Hostus is a hero in search of his epic poet. But he has mistaken his script; firstly, this 'fair son of an unworthy father' (12.346) is more of a Lausus to a Mezentius than an Ascanius to an Aeneas, that is to say that he is cast in the role of one of the doomed Virgilian father and son teams who die without heirs. Secondly, Hostus does indeed find his epic poet, but in his earlier career as warrior, one who offers death rather than eternal fame. The scene that ensues is a reworking of that in *Aeneid* 9 in which Apollo gives his blessing to Ascanius' killing of Remulus Numanus, the scene that functions as *rite de passage* for Ascanius and gives divine guarantee of the continuity of the Julian family. In Silius the epic poet takes the place of epic hero: Apollo intervenes, as god of poetry to prophesy Ennius' future career as the first Latin epic poet, and as avenging archer-god to shoot an arrow through Hostus' temples. The Virgilian scene had earlier been used by Silius at 4.454–79 when Mars congratulates Scipio Africanus on rescuing his father, setting his divine seal on the preservation of father by son.[49] In book 12 the diversion of the model from epic hero to poet reveals clearly how epic success, in the sense of successful deeds of valour successfully preserved for posterity, depends on the proper succession of both hero and poet. Virgil's Apollo tells Ascanius that his is 'the path to the stars'; this will be the reward of the successful line of Aeneas. Silius' Apollo promises that Ennius 'will exalt Roman generals to the sky' (12.411) (while the Sardinian leader Hampsagoras 'follows his son's footsteps to the shades' (12.419), which may also be understood figuratively of the future obscurity of this line), and Ennius will do this because he is the Latin successor to the great Greek poet Hesiod (12.410–13). Homer might have been expected, but Hesiod is chosen partly perhaps because the Dream of Homer at the beginning of the *Annals* is modelled ultimately on Hesiod's meeting with the Muses at the beginning of the *Theogony*, but more importantly because 'the Ascraean old man',

[49] See p. 97 above.

Hesiod, is one of the great poetic ancestors of Gallus in the scene of poetic initiation and succession at the end of Virgil's sixth *Eclogue*. By his imitation of the Virgilian Ascanius and Apollo episode, Silius makes a claim for his own poetic ancestor that is as confident and proud as the claim Ennius makes for himself in the Dream of Homer.

If the survivor Iulus is the model for Ennius, the tragic Marcellus is the model for Silius' Homer, whose ghost Scipio sees in the necromancy of book 13.778–97. There are dense verbal echoes of the Marcellus passage in *Aeneid* 6, and the traditionally aged figure of Homer has surprisingly turned into a youth (*iuuenis* 13.779; of Marcellus *Aen*. 6.861), to join the ranks of the Virgilian young men of great promise but thwarted of the full realization of their potential by death. Unlike the white worn by the priests and poets in Virgil's Elysian fields (*Aen*. 6.665), Homer's headband is purple, the colour of youth and death. Homer's actual achievement is not denied (he is the poet who sang of the whole universe), but it is past and partial. Scipio tells the Sibyl that he would think him a god, were he not in the darkness of the Underworld (784–5); the Sibyl replies in perfect tenses 'he *deserved* to seem a god,[50] and there *was* no small divinity in his great breast' (786–7). There is paradox in talking of the eternal divine in past tenses. Homer's poetry is of universal spatial scope: he had a mental vision of the Underworld, before he actually saw it after death, which he revealed on Earth, and he exalted Troy to the stars. But the endless stretch of time eluded him (in this he is less successful than Statius' Amphiaraus who was not debarred through demotion to the Underworld from clear vision of events on earth in the present). Scipio, echoing the lament of Alexander the Great that he did not have Homer to celebrate his deeds, wishes that fate would allow Homer to sing of Rome; the language he uses is that in which Anchises regrets that harsh fate will cut off Marcellus before he realizes his promise. Marcellus' death cheats the elder Marcellus and his descendants (*Aen*. 6.864 *nepotum*); Homer's death cheats future generations of Romans (*Pun*. 13.795 *nepotes*) of epic magnification of Roman history. Generational continuity matters both for the subjects of epic and for its readers.

The reader, however, will set off Scipio's pessimism against Apollo's promise to Ennius in the previous book; Rome has already in its midst a man with the power to write a Latin epic adequate to succeed the Greek

---

[50] 13.786 *meruit deus esse uideri;* cf. the 'divine' honours paid to Ennius by Silius at 12.392.

predecessors. Scipio's unwitting use of Virgil's words reveals to the reader the continued succession after Ennius – dare one say down to Silius?

The 'anxiety of influence'

Harold Bloom's theory of the relationship between poets and their predecessors, to which he gives the name the 'anxiety of influence',[51] has been something of a godsend to critics of ancient literature with their traditionally historical approach to their texts. Here is a theory that, in contrast to the ahistorical or even antihistorical tendencies of formalism, structuralism and some post-structuralism, puts a historical relationship back at the centre of modern theory. Bloom's own sources are a bricolage that includes modern depth psychology and Jewish mysticism, but also classical and neoclassical literary theory and practice. Bloom's single most important predecessor among modern critical studies is perhaps Walter Jackson Bate's *The Burden of the Past and the English Poet*,[52] which discusses the anxiety of eighteenth-century neoclassical writers about their ability to equal the great creative achievement of the previous century. Bate looks forward to the importance for the Romantics of the ideas of 'originality' and 'sincerity', developed under this pressure; but there is a close analogy between the self-conscious 'inferiority' of the eighteenth century and the first century A.D. awareness of a 'decline' with respect to the great authors of the later Republic and Augustan period, a critical construction that has all too often been taken at face value by modern classicists rather than seen for what it is, a moralizing and nostalgic fiction that need contain no more truth (or untruth) than the related fictions of moral and political decline.

There are a number of reasons why Bloom's theory is particularly attractive for students of ancient epic. Firstly, the theory is presented initially in terms of an allegorical reading of an epic, *Paradise Lost*.[53] Milton's Satan is the figure of the 'strong poet', falling away from his father in rebellion and attempting to establish an independence in the intolerable knowledge of the overwhelming power of his creator. For Bloom Milton himself is not a poet of this kind, being a superhuman figure immune from such anxiety; yet this reading in Milton's epic narrative of a poetics, or poetic (auto-)biography, is very much in line

---

[51] Bloom (1973).   [52] Bate (1971).   [53] Bloom (1973), 20 ff.

with an important tendency of Miltonic criticism to read the objective narrative of *Paradise Lost* as a subjective account of the narrator's – and reader's – experience. The ability to read in this way is undoubtedly the result of the fact that the poem tells a story which is the story of Everyman, insofar as Christianity teaches that every Christian lives out in his or her own life the historical Fall and Redemption; but Milton also exploits a self-reflexive quality present, as we have seen, in the epic from its origins and accentuated in the Latin epic. There is a strong similarity between *Paradise Lost* and Lucretius' *De rerum natura* in the way that the narrated (or the expounded), the narrator and the reader all merge into one another, but Lucretius too is deeply enmeshed in the workings of epic and his didactic poem in turn significantly affected the subsequent course of Latin epic.

Secondly, Bloom's theory reinstates a psychological, almost biographical approach to the relationship between texts, dramatizing a struggle between Titanic individual writers rather than allowing for a more diffused intertextuality where text speaks to text rather than subject to subject. There are a number of features of the ancient genre of epic that make the subjectivity of Bloom's account rather appealing. It is a genre that is almost defined by an individual author, Homer, the great father figure not only of later epic poetry but of Greek culture as a whole. Elevated by his idolaters almost to the status of the father of the gods, whose thoughts as omniscient narrator he shared already, Homer becomes both the great source and fountain-head for all later writers and also the boundless Ocean that threatens to swamp the latecomer. This is the language of Bloom: 'The precursors flood us, and our imaginations can die by drowning in them, but no imaginative life is possible if such inundation is wholly evaded.'[54] But the imagery of poetic rivers and seas is also that of the Alexandrian poets, chief among whom Callimachus, whose poetics is based on the presupposition that it is artistic death to attempt direct imitation of Homer; and Alexandrian poetics is where Virgil comes from. Homer is a father as well as the Ocean; Bloom's central model for the relationship between poetic fathers and sons is the Oedipus complex; the Latin epics treat succession both of heroes (emperors) and poets in terms of a smooth or violent transmission within the family.

Thirdly, Bloom is also Alexandrian in his contention that there is no

[54] Bloom (1973), 154.

clear distinction between poetic creation and criticism.[55] 'As literary history lengthens, all poetry necessarily becomes verse-criticism, just as all criticism becomes prose–poetry.'[56] The second half of this formulation might have puzzled Callimachus, but the first half would not. Of the ancient genres epic was the most intensively commented upon; the (prose) commentators on Homer fed into Virgil's poetic creation in the *Aeneid*, and the epics after Virgil are also Alexandrian in being verse commentaries on the *Aeneid*.[57]

Fourthly, Bloom's understanding of poetic succession as a struggle leads to the centrality of antithesis as a relationship between earlier and later poets and texts. 'Opposition in imitation', or 'contrast imitation', has long been recognized as an important kind of imitation in antiquity, becoming especially self-conscious with the Alexandrian poets. The revaluation of epic heroism and other values so apparent in *Paradise Lost* is a late example of what achieves the status almost of a law of Latin epic, where this adversarial kind of imitation is practised on a vast scale. The most striking example is Lucan's negative rewriting of the *Aeneid*, but the *Aeneid* itself already inverts its models, establishing alternative modes of heroism to those of the Homeric epics, and more emphatically inverting the values of Lucretius' 'epic' didactic. Silius' *Punica* has been described as an anti-*Pharsalia*, restoring the positive Roman values savaged by Lucan rather as Virgil restores the traditional values that had been inverted by Lucretius.

The example of Lucretius should make us beware of translating Bloom's theory too literally to the Roman world. Lucretius' antithetical stance to his predecessors comes in the first place out of a philosophical tradition of polemical inversion that confronts abstract systems rather than personalities (although one might want to go on and suggest that ancient *odium philosophicum* had something to do with the close, almost family-like relations between philosophers). There are other ways of dealing with poetic rivalry than the Oedipal; images of a poetic competition conducted with good humour are common enough in antiquity, though the Bloomian might well wish to distinguish between manifest and hidden content in these images. In the case of epic we also

---

[55] Bloom (1975), 34 for an explicit reference to the situation in antiquity.

[56] *Ibid.*, 3.

[57] In this respect too *Paradise Lost* is a highly classicizing epic: '*Paradise Lost* remains, when all is said and done, the finest commentary on Virgil's *Aeneid* ever written' (Harding (1962), 134).

have to reckon with the fact that images of a respectful and peaceful succession from poetic father to son are at least as easy to discern as more violent acts of appropriation. But the relationship always threatens to become uneasy, because the poet, as much as his heroes, is involved in a power-game for high stakes. If the hero must strive to be the best, or to win the world for his throne, the poet is always challenged to be supreme in the supreme genre. Telemachus and Ascanius are faithful sons, but, in the need to be warned off shooting the father's bow[58] or winning the war in Latium in the father's absence, we perhaps catch the ever-present desire and its attendant anxiety.

[58] See Goldhill (1984), 189–91.

Bibliography

Ahl, F. M. (1976) *Lucan: An Introduction*. Ithaca and London
  (1986) 'Statius' *Thebaid*: a reconsideration', *ANRW* II. 32.5, 2803–912
Ahl, F. M., Davis, M. A. and Pomeroy, A. (1986) 'Silius Italicus' *ANRW* II. 32.4, 2492–561
Alföldi, A. (1974) *Die Struktur des voretruskischen Römerstaates*. Heidelberg
Bandera, C. (1981) 'Sacrificial levels in Virgil's *Aeneid*', *Arethusa* 14, 217–39
Barchiesi, A. (1991) 'Discordant Muses', *PCPhS* 37, 1–21
Bassett, E. L. (1966) 'Hercules and the hero of the *Punica*', in L. Wallach (ed.) *The Classical Tradition: Literary and Historical Studies in Honor of H. Caplan*. Ithaca and New York, 258–73
Bate, W. J. (1971) *The Burden of the Past and the English Poet*. London
Beard, M. and North, J. (eds.) (1990) *Pagan Priests*. London
Beye, C. R. (1982) *Epic and Romance in the* Argonautica *of Apollonius*. Carbondale
Bloom, H. (1973) *The Anxiety of Influence: A Theory of Poetry*. New York and London
  (1975) *A Map of Misreading*. New York and London
Bonds, W. S. (1985) 'Two combats in the *Thebaid*', *TAPhA* 115, 225–35
Bono, B. J. (1984) *Literary Transvaluation. From Vergilian Epic to Shakespearean Tragicomedy*. Berkeley, Los Angeles, London
Boyle, A. J. (ed.) (1988) *The Imperial Muse. Ramus Essays on Roman Literature of the Empire*. I *To Juvenal through Ovid*. Berwick, Victoria
  (ed.) (1990) *The Imperial Muse. Ramus Essays on Roman Literature of the Empire*. II *Flavian Epicist to Claudian*. Bendigo
  (ed.) (1993) *Roman Epic*. London
Brenk, F. E. (1988) 'Wind and waves, sacrifice and treachery: Diodorus, Appian and the death of Palinurus in Vergil', *Aevum* 62, 69–80
Brink, C. O. (1972) 'Ennius and the Hellenistic worship of Homer', *AJPh* 93, 547–67
Brissenden, R. F. and Eade, J. C. (eds.) (1976) *Studies in the Eighteenth Century* III. Canberra
Brooks, P. (1985) *Reading for the Plot*. New York 1985
Buchheit, V. (1971) 'Epikurs Triumph des Geistes (Lucr. 1.62–79)', *Hermes* 99, 303–23
  (1972) *Der Anspruch des Dichters in Vergils Georgika: Dichtertum und Heilsweg*. Impulse der Forschung 8, Darmstadt

Burkert, W. (1979) *Structure and History in Greek Mythology and Ritual*. Berkeley, Los Angeles, London

(1985) *Greek Religion: Archaic and Classical*, trans. J. Raffan. Oxford

Chambers, A. B. (1963) 'Chaos in *Paradise Lost*', *JHI* 24 (1963), 55–84

Cornell, T. J. (1975) 'Aeneas and the twins: the development of the Roman foundation legend, *PCPhS* n.s. 21, 1–32

Dauge, Y. A. (1981) *Le Barbare: recherches sur la conception romaine de la barbarie et de la civilisation*. Coll. Latomus 176, Brussels

Detienne, M. (1981) 'Between beasts and gods', in Gordon (1981), 215–28

Dupont, F. (1989) 'The emperor-god's other body', in Feher (1989), 396–419

Durling, R. M. (1965) *The Figure of the Poet in the Renaissance*. Cambridge, MA

Feeney, D. C. (1986a) '*Stat magni nominis umbra*. Lucan on the greatness of Pompeius Magnus', *CQ* n.s. 36, 239–43

(1986b) 'History and revelation in Vergil's Underworld', *PCPhS* n.s. 32, 1–24

(1991) *The Gods in Epic: Poets and Critics of the Classical Tradition*. Oxford

Feher, M. (1989) *Fragments for a History of the Human Body* III. New York

Foley, H. P. (1985) *Ritual Irony: Poetry and Sacrifice in Euripides*. Ithaca and London

Fontenrose, J. (1959) *Python*. Berkeley, Los Angeles, London

Fowler, A. (1964) *Spenser and the Numbers of Time*. London

Fowler, D. P. (1987) 'Vergil on killing virgins', in Whitby *et al.* (1987), 185–98

Fränkel, H. (1975) *Early Greek Poetry and Philosophy*, trans. M. Hadas and J. Willis. Oxford

Frye, N. (1963) 'The structure of imagery in *The Faerie Queene*', in *Fables of Identity: Studies in Poetic Mythology*. New York, 69–87

Gatz, B. (1967) *Weltalter, goldene Zeit und sinnverwandte Vorstellungen*. Spudasmata 16, Hildesheim

Girard, R. (1977) *Violence and the Sacred*, trans. P. Gregory. Baltimore and London

Goff, B. E. (1990) *The Noose of Words. Readings of Desire, Violence and Language in Euripides' Hippolytus*. Cambridge.

Goldhill, S. (1984) *Language, Sexuality, Narrative: The* Oresteia. Cambridge

(1991) *The Poet's Voice. Essays on Poetics and Greek Literature*. Cambridge

Gordon, R. L. (ed.) (1981) *Myth, Religion & Society. Structuralist Essays by M. Detienne, L. Gernet, J.-P. Vernant & P. Vidal-Naquet*. Cambridge

(1990) 'The veil of power', in Beard and North (1990), 201–31

Greenblatt, S. (1980) *Renaissance Self-fashioning. From More to Shakespeare*. Chicago and London

Griffin, J. (1985) 'The creation of characters in the *Aeneid*', in *Latin Poets and Roman Life*. London, 183 97

Grottanelli, C. (1972) 'I connotati fenici della morte di Elissa', *Religione e Civiltà* 1, 319–27

Hardie, P. R. (1986) *Virgil's* Aeneid: *Cosmos and Imperium*. Oxford

(1990a) 'Ovid's Theban history: the first "Anti-*Aeneid*"?', *CQ* n.s 40, 224–35

(1990b) 'Flavian epicists on Virgil's epic technique', in Boyle (1990), 3–20

(1991a) 'The *Aeneid* and the *Oresteia*', *PVS* 20, 29–45

(1991b) 'The masks of Dido', *Omnibus* 21, 12–14

(1991c) 'The Janus episode in Ovid's *Fasti*', *MD* 26, 47–64

(1992) 'Augustan poets on the mutability of Rome' in Powell (1992), 59–82

(1993a) 'After Rome II: Renaissance epic', in Boyle (1993), ch.14

(1993b) 'Tales of unity and division in imperial latin epic', in Molyneux (1993)

Harding, D. P. (1962) *The Club of Hercules: Studies in the Classical Background of Paradise Lost*. Urbana

Harries, B. (1990) 'The spinner and the poet: Arachne in Ovid's *Metamorphoses*', *PCPhS* n.s. 36, 64–82

(1991) 'Ovid and the Fabii: *Fasti* 2.193–474', *CQ* n.s. 41, 150–68

Henderson, J. G. W. (1988) 'Lucan/the word at war', in Boyle (1988), 122–64

(1991) 'Statius' *Thebaid*/form premade', *PCPhS* n.s. 37, 30–80

Hinds, S. (1987) *The Metamorphosis of Persephone: Ovid and the Self-conscious Muse*. Cambridge

Hubert, H. and Mauss, M. (1964) *Sacrifice: Its Nature and Function*, trans. W. D. Halls. London

Kantorowicz, E. H. (1957) *The King's Two Bodies. A Study in Mediaeval Political Theology*. Princeton

Kepple, L. R. (1976) 'Arruns and the death of Aeneas', *AJPh* 97, 344–60

Klinnert, T. C. (1970) *Capaneus-Hippomedon. Interpretationen zur Heldendarstellung in der Thebais des P. Papinius Statius*. Diss. Heidelberg

Leach, E. W. (1974) 'Ekphrasis and the theme of artistic failure in Ovid's *Metamorphoses*', *Ramus* 3, 102–42

Lossau, M. (1980) 'Elpenor und Palinurus', *WS* n.f. 14, 102–24

Lowenstam, S. (1981) *The Death of Patroklos: A Study in Typology*. Beitr. z. kl. Phil. 133, Königstein

Lyne, R. O. A. M. (1987) *Further Voices in Vergil's* Aeneid. Oxford

McGuire, D. T. (1990) 'Textual strategies and political suicide in Flavian epic', in Boyle (1990), 21–45

Maltby, R. (1991) *A Lexicon of Ancient Latin Etymologies*. Leeds

Masters, J. M. (1992) *Poetry and Civil War in Lucan's* Bellum Civile. Cambridge

Molyneux, J. H. (ed.) (1993) *Nottingham Classical Literature Studies*, 1. Nottingham

Murrin, M. (1980) *The Allegorical Epic. Essays in its Rise and Decline*. Chicago and London

Nagy, G. (1979) *The Best of the Achaeans*. Baltimore and London

Newman, J. K. (1986) *The Classical Epic Tradition*. Wisconsin

Nicoll, W. S. M. (1988) 'The sacrifice of Palinurus', *CQ* n.s. 38, 459–72

O'Hara, J. J. (1990) *Death and the Optimistic Prophecy in Vergil's* Aeneid. Princeton

O'Higgins, D. (1988) 'Lucan as *vates*', *CA* 7, 208–26

Parker, P. A. (1979) *Inescapable Romance: Studies in the Poetics of a Mode*. Princeton

Pascal, C. B. (1990) 'The dubious devotion of Turnus', *TAPhA* 120, 251–68

Pomeroy, A. J. (1990) 'Silius Italicus as "doctus poeta"', in Boyle (1990), 119–39

Powell, A. (1992) *Roman Poetry and Propaganda in the Age of Augustus*. Bristol

Putnam, M. C. J. (1965) *The Poetry of the* Aeneid. *Four Studies in Imaginative Unity and Design*. Cambridge, MA and London

Quint, D. (1989) 'Epic and empire', *CL* 41, 1–32

(1991) 'Repetition and ideology in the *Aeneid*', *MD* 24. 9–54

Renger, C. (1985) *Aeneas und Turnus: Analyse einer Feindschaft*. Studien zur klassischen Philologie 11, Frankfurt am Main

Ricks, C. (1976) 'Allusion: the poet as heir', in Brissenden and Eade (1976), 209–40

Rieks, R. (1967) *Homo, Humanus, Humanitas. Zur Humanität in der lateinischen Literatur des ersten nachchristlichen Jahrhunderts*. Munich

Rosati, G. (1983) *Narciso e Pigmalione: Illusione e spettacolo nelle Metamorfosi di Ovidio*. Florence

Sansone, D. (1988) *Greek Athletics and the Genesis of Sport*. Berkeley, Los Angeles, London

Schetter, W. (1960) *Untersuchungen zur epischen Kunst des Statius*. Wiesbaden

Schwartz, R. M. (1988) *Remembering and Repeating. Biblical Creation in* Paradise Lost. Cambridge

Segal, C. (1986) 'Greek tragedy and society', in *Interpreting Greek Tragedy. Myth, Poetry, Text*. Ithaca and London, 21–47

Shoaf, R. A. (1985) *Milton, Poet of Duality. A Study of Semiosis in the Poetry and the Prose*. New Haven and London

Solodow, J. B. (1988) *The World of Ovid's* Metamorphoses. Chapel Hill and London

Steadman, J. M. (1967) *Milton and the Renaissance Hero*. Oxford

Suerbaum, W. (1972) '*Poeta laureatus et triumphans*. Die Dichterkrönung Petrarcas und sein Ennius-Bild', *Poetica* 5, 293–328

Taran, S. L. (1985) 'εἰσὶ τρίχες: an erotic motif in the *Greek Anthology*', *JHS* 105, 90–107

Tupet, A.-M. (1970) 'Dido magicienne', *REL* 48, 229–58

van Brock, N. (1959) 'Substitution rituelle', *RHA* 65, 117–46

Vernant, J.-P. (1981) 'Sacrificial and alimentary codes in Hesiod', in Gordon (1981), 57–79

Versnel, H. S. (1970) *Triumphus*. Leiden

    (1981) 'Self-sacrifice, compensation, anonymous gods', in *Le Sacrifice dans l'antiquité*. Entret. Hardt 27, Geneva, 135–94

Vessey, D. (1974) 'Silius Italicus on the fall of Saguntum', *CPh* 69, 28–36

Weinstock, S. (1971) *Divus Julius*. Oxford

Whitby, M., Hardie, P. and Whitby, M. (eds.) (1987) *Homo Viator. Classical Essays for John Bramble*. Bristol

Whitman, C. H. (1958) *Homer and the Heroic Tradition*. Cambridge, MA.

Williams, G. (1978) *Change and Decline: Roman Literature in the Early Empire*. Berkeley, Los Angeles, London

Zeitlin, F. I. (1982) *Under the Sign of the Shield: Semiotics and Aeschylus'* Seven against Thebes. Rome

General index

Index of passages discussed